P9-CRV-891

The Infodemic
How Censorship and Lies Made the World Sicker and Less Free

COLUMBIA GLOBAL REPORTS
NEW YORK

The Infodemic
How Censorship and Lies Made the World Sicker and Less Free

Joel Simon and
Robert Mahoney

The Infodemic
How Censorship and Lies Made the World Sicker and Less Free
Copyright © 2022 by Joel Simon and Robert Mahoney

Published by Columbia Global Reports
91 Claremont Avenue, Suite 515
New York, NY 10027
globalreports.columbia.edu
facebook.com/columbiaglobalreports
@columbiaGR

Library of Congress Cataloging-in-Publication Data

Names: Simon, Joel, 1964- author. Mahoney, Robert —author.
Title: The infodemic : how censorship and lies made the world sicker and
  less free / Joel Simon and Robert Mahoney.
Description: New York : Columbia Global Reports, [2022] | Includes
  bibliographical references.
Identifiers: LCCN 2021059233 (print) | LCCN 2021059234 (ebook) | ISBN
  9781735913681 (Paperback) | ISBN 9781735913698 (eBook)
Subjects: LCSH: Communication in politics. | Communication in public
  health. | COVID-19 (Disease)--Government policy--Case studies. | Civil
  rights--Political aspects. | Censorship.
Classification: LCC JA85 .S536 2022 (print) | LCC JA85 (ebook) | DDC
  320.01/4--dc23/eng/20220107
LC record available at https://lccn.loc.gov/2021059233
LC ebook record available at https://lccn.loc.gov/2021059234

Book design by Strick&Williams
Map design by Jeffrey L. Ward

Printed in the United States of America

CONTENTS

Introduction

This book chronicles the way in which censorship was deployed in countries around the world in response to an unprecedented threat to public health. Alongside the COVID-19 pandemic, there was an infodemic, a deluge of lies, distortions, and bungled communication that obliterated the truth. This infodemic did not spring from thin air. By suppressing the news and manipulating the public, governments helped fuel the infodemic, and then exploited it to deflect criticism and consolidate power. It was not just misinformation that undermined the global response to the COVID-19 pandemic. It was censorship.

It was censorship that turned a terrible disease into an assault on rights, as governments suppressed not just speech but a broad range of political activities. Instead of communicating openly with citizens, governments suppressed critical information or actively misled or confused their citizens, a strategy that has been dubbed "censorship through noise." In response to the pandemic, many governments increased surveillance, in some cases introducing new technologies that

offered limited public health benefits but allowed authorities to
track people's every move. In democracies, governments relied
on a more sophisticated and increasingly effective means of
censorship, drowning the truth in a sea of lies. The intersection
of new communication technologies, declining public trust,
and collapsing local media made these techniques exceedingly
effective. The result is that people around the world are not only
less healthy. They are less free.

Despite their vastly different experiences with COVID-19
and their different political systems, most governments were
united in a shared desire to downplay the threat of the disease
and cover up their own incompetence. In order to succeed, they
had to silence the experts and censor the independent journalists who amplified their voices. As a disease, COVID-19
was uniquely suited to such an endeavor. The symptoms often
matched those of a bad flu, and the most severely afflicted were
the elderly and people with underlying health conditions—
meaning that ravages of the disease could be camouflaged or
hidden from public view, at least for a period. The dynamic
played out differently in different countries depending on the
nature of the political system, the level of infection, and the
characteristics of the country's political leaders. But the game
plan was remarkably similar: suppress, marginalize, minimize,
undermine, deny, and confuse.

COVID-19 first emerged in China, one of the most heavily
censored places on Earth. China covered up the initial outbreak by silencing doctors and by hunting down and jailing the
small group of independent bloggers who documented events in
Wuhan. From China, censorship spread along with the disease
to Iran, Egypt, Russia, and across the authoritarian world, where

12   governments not only suppressed critical coverage but used the public health emergency as a pretext to usurp power, implementing new laws limiting assembly and speech. In populist-led democracies—Brazil, India, and the US—governments relied less on brute repression and more on the techniques of modern censorship, which involves confusing and manipulating the public by discrediting and undermining independent voices. Misinformation is a tool of the new censorship, but it is also a by-product, as rumors, lies, and distortions fill the void when governments mislead the public. The pressure on social media companies to curb the spread of misinformation on their platforms was an understandable response when lies were literally killing people, but empowering Facebook, YouTube, and Twitter to remove political speech may ultimately play into the hands of the state. It's all part of a global political shift in which governments increasingly have the upper hand.

It was censorship—both the crude and the modern kind—that made it possible for governments to undermine public trust while asserting new powers. But of course governments needed to consider the use of certain authorities in order to fight the pandemic, including restricting movement, and implementing mask and vaccine mandates. While the legitimacy of such efforts provided cover for governments that sought to use their expanded powers to curb dissent, it also made it difficult for defenders of civil liberties to draw a bright line between necessary restrictions and those that were excessive or opportunistic.

One framework for evaluating the legitimacy of government actions during the pandemic is to determine whether they were legal. Under international law, governments have the right to impose temporary restrictions or even suspend certain rights in response to threats to public health. To do so legally, they must first declare a state of emergency, and show why severe restrictions are necessary. The problem with relying on such international legal standards is that most governments do not abide by them even during the best of times. Because the COVID-19 pandemic represented a clear threat to public health, one requiring government intervention, some actions taken by governments may have been legitimate but not legal. Others, conversely, may have been legal but not legitimate.

The most nuanced framework for evaluating restrictions on freedom in the context of the pandemic is positive and negative liberty. This concept, as developed by the philosopher Isaiah Berlin, is sometimes expressed as *freedom to* and *freedom from*. Berlin outlined his ideas in a series of lectures delivered at the height of the Cold War and later assembled in a 1969 volume entitled *Four Essays on Liberty*. There is an "open war that is being fought between two systems of ideas which return different and conflicting answers to what has long been the central question of politics—the question of obedience and coercion," Berlin wrote. "Why should I (or anyone) obey anyone else? Why should I not live as I like? Must I obey? If I disobey, may I be coerced? By whom and to what degree, and in the name of what, and for the sake of what?"

Negative liberty, in its most reductive sense, is freedom from government constraint. All people must be protected against a range of government intrusion on their physical person and into their ideas and thoughts. Positive liberty, on the other hand, is the ability to shape the destiny of their own society and live by its laws. Both negative liberty and positive

14   liberty are essential, but they sometimes conflict. For example, the original US Constitution provided a blueprint for the exercise of democracy, including legal protections against intrusive government power. It also preserved and sanctified the most egregious violation of negative liberty, slavery. The concept of positive liberty can also be abused. Totalitarian and authoritarian forms of government generally justify their exercise of power, including imposing restrictions on political participation, in order to achieve some worthy social purpose—ensuring economic growth, providing more equitable distribution of resources, or defending against an external threat.

Applying Berlin's framework to the debate about COVID-19 and mask-wearing, the writer and philosopher Kwame Anthony Appiah noted "the trouble is that we usually don't think hard enough about all that's actually required to live free," adding, "There's precious little freedom in the sick ward and less still in the graveyard." Also drawing on Berlin's framework, as well as their experience as a Russian emigré and their research on the threat of creeping authoritarianism, *New Yorker* writer Masha Gessen argued that, "For a sense of common cause to appear, there has to be a sense of *us*: a community that is facing a threat and mounting a response. But we have vastly different experiences of the pandemic and vastly different expectations of the government."

To boil down Berlin's argument and place it in the context of the pandemic, the legitimacy of a government's efforts to restrict negative liberty is derived from the existence of positive liberty, as expressed through the consent of the governed. The right to speak, to listen, to express and exchange ideas, to communicate closely held beliefs, to criticize authorities, to demand account-ability: these are the broad range of activities enabled by posi-tive liberty. The act of censorship is thus a direct assault on the most precious form of freedom, and opens the door to broader restrictions on fundamental rights. In other words, in order to assess the legitimacy of a specific government action taken during the pandemic one must examine not the action itself, but the broader context. Restrictions on positive liberty, even severe ones such as lockdowns, are legitimized through the existence of positive liberty, in which the people impacted are able to express their views, and ultimately if they so wish to compel the government to change course. Restrictions imposed under a veil of censorship are never fully legitimate even when they achieve their stated purpose of protecting public health. In making any judgments about the legitimacy of state action in the context of the pandemic, one must look at both positive and negative liberty and understand the ways in which they interact.

The relationship between the pandemic, censorship, and the assault on rights may be counterintuitive, especially to those in the United States who experienced a deluge of infor-mation rather than a drought. But any confusion is based on a misunderstanding of how modern censorship works, and how it is linked to state power. The Soviet Union was built around a top-down information management system that allowed the government to impose a single narrative in the absence of any independent voices. Today, even in China, people have access to enormous quantities of information and a range of views. China readily deploys the repressive power of the state, but even there, day-to-day censorship more often consists of drowning out and controlling competing voices so that the government narrative

16   prevails. Strategies can include manipulating social media; controlling traditional media through regulation and advertising pressure; and orchestrating state-sponsored harassment campaigns to undermine and marginalize critics. The result is the same one achieved in the Soviet Union, which is the triumph of the government narrative. Once the narrative is set, then other restrictions on rights are easier to achieve.

The Infodemic explains how the manipulation of information opened the door to an assault on rights as well as the independent institutions, including the media, that ensure accountability. It tells the story of how the pandemic changed the world not as a result of the disease itself but because of political leaders' response. As the threat to public health recedes, these politically charged changes risk becoming the pandemic's legacy. It's a future we can avoid only if we are willing to stand up for our right to speak freely.

Censored in China

Talking always came naturally to Chen Qiushi. Growing up as an only child in China's remote and frigid Daxinganling prefecture bordering Russia, Chen wanted to be an actor. He also wanted to be on television. His mother pushed him to study law, which he did at Heilongjiang University. But he also took courses on drama and broadcasting. After graduating from college, he hosted a local talk show in his spare time.

In 2007, Chen moved to Beijing, and after passing China's equivalent of the bar exam, he took a job at the prestigious Longan law firm. His focus on media, broadcasting, and internet law earned him the nickname "cultural lawyer." After work, he dabbled in stand-up comedy at local bars and did voice acting. He also loved being a contestant on TV programs, including *I Am a Speaker*, a talent show for orators modeled on *The Voice*. Panels of judges evaluated contestants on diction, message, and expression. His final performance on the show was on "the power of speech." Chen contrasted censorship in Nazi Germany with Thomas Jefferson's commitment to free expression

18   as embodied in the First Amendment of the US Constitution.
"A country can only grow stronger when it is accompanied by
critics," Chen proclaimed. "Only freedom of expression and the
freedom of press can protect a country from descending into a
place where the weak are preyed upon by the strong." Chen was
awarded second place.

Chen used the renown generated by his television appearances to build a formidable social media following. He asked
prominent journalists to coach him and help him hone his
delivery. In 2018, he uploaded more than four hundred short
videos that provided a basic tutorial on Chinese law. He gained
more than 1.5 million followers on TikTok, making him the
most popular "legal" personality on the entire platform.

During a speech to university students, Chen recalled that
he had only studied law to please his mother and that his true
passion was journalism. Being on TV was not just a lifelong
aspiration. It made him proud. But Chen was also committed
to something more profound. He wanted to bear witness. He
wanted to tell the truth.

In the summer of 2019, as street protests exploded across Hong
Kong, Chen got his chance. The protests were sparked by a new
extradition bill that subjected Hong Kongers to criminal prosecution in mainland China for offenses against national security. After three activists who participated in the 2014 protests
known as the Umbrella Movement were sentenced to jail, thousands of Hong Kongers poured into the streets to express their
disdain. Chen wanted to know more, but had no confidence in
the accounts he was reading in the Chinese media. He flew from
Beijing to Hong Kong on August 17, armed with a smartphone

and a commitment to honestly report what he saw. Chen was
thirty-four and single, with no one waiting for him at home.

The Umbrella Movement had begun when Hong Kong students occupied buildings throughout the city to protest the
erosion of democracy and the increasing influence of Beijing.
Under the 1997 handover agreement, China had pledged to
maintain civil rights, an independent judiciary, and capitalism
in the former British colony, a commitment that was codified in
the Basic Law. While the Basic Law represented a binding international agreement, it also reflected the realities of the moment,
namely that Hong Kong was an economic engine for all of China,
a manufacturing hub and the center for direct foreign investment that the mainland needed. Hong Kong also occupied a
separate information landscape from the rest of China. Free-
wheeling Hong Kong newspapers, with their unfettered political coverage and criticism of the authorities, did not circulate
on the mainland and thus the threat of "ideological" contamina-
tion was easier to contain.

But the calculus for Beijing had changed in the intervening
two decades. As manufacturing exploded inside China and the
country was integrated into the global economy, Hong Kong's
special status became less critical. Meanwhile, the internet and
social media had created a blended information environment,
and the Communist government struggled to contain ideas that
emerged in Hong Kong from spreading to the mainland. China,
under its nationalist and authoritarian leader Xi Jinping, began
to assert greater control over Hong Kong, pushing the boundaries of its international commitments.

The spark for the protesters was Beijing's perceived inter-
ference in Hong Kong's 2014 elections, namely ham-handed

20   efforts by the Chinese Communist Party to pre-screen candidates for Hong Kong's Chief Executive, the city's top official.
The initial protests faded after seventy-nine days, but resent-
ments festered. Five years later, sparked by crude efforts to ram
through the extradition bill, Hong Kongers once again had taken
to the streets.

Chen used his first video on August 17 to introduce himself and explain his approach. "Why am I in Hong Kong?" Chen
asked as he stared directly into the camera, wearing a green
Day-Glo safety vest over a white T-shirt, the city's skyline as
his backdrop. "Because Hong Kong is quite chaotic." Chen con-
fessed that journalism was a hobby of sorts, but that he still
had an obligation "to be present" when and where news was
unfolding. He also pledged to be objective. "I won't express my
opinion carelessly," Chen promised. "I won't say who I support
or who I disagree with. I wish to leave behind my own prejudice and treat everything with neutrality. Because I am not sat-
isfied with the public opinion and media environment in China,
I decided to come to Hong Kong and become the media myself."

As he wandered the city, Chen observed that people in
Hong Kong were still "living their normal happy lives" despite
the protests. He picked up copies of the local newspapers
noting that while he could read them online from the mainland
this would involve bypassing the Chinese government firewall,
which was illegal. "I am a lawyer and should not break any law,"
Chen acknowledged.

Chen's video reports showed him attending rallies, and featured an occasional interview. But he mostly spoke straight to
the camera, his tone friendly but emphatic, exuding the youthful
confidence of the kind of pedantic student who dominates

classroom discussions. Trim, with a thick pompadour of dark   21
hair and an elongated face, Chen sported a sparse mustache and
goatee that encircled his mouth, from which emerged a cascade
of words, tirelessly and effortlessly.

Chen described how the accounts of the protests in the
Hong Kong media sharply contrasted the version of events provided on the mainland. A girl hit in the eye with a rubber bullet?
Hong Kong media said she was fired on by police while Chinese state media blamed her injury on protesters. (Where did
they get a gun and a rubber bullet? Chen asked rhetorically.) The
mainland journalist who was beaten by an angry mob at the airport? Hong Kong media reported he was actually a state security
agent. The men with white shirts and clubs who were rampaging
and attacking the protesters? Chinese media described them as
patriotic youth. Hong Kong media called them gang members
recruited as paid goons.

"Under the circumstances where information is so confusing, we especially need to absorb all information that's available and not just parts of it," Chen observed. "Only by collecting
and cross-referencing enough information will we be able to
understand the true facts."

On his second day in Hong Kong, Chen attended two rallies, the
first organized by pro-democracy protesters, and the second by
a group that had come together to express their support for the
police. Chen spoke with several dozen people and found plenty
of differences, but also a shared love for Hong Kong and an
appreciation for material benefits that the city provides, from
health care to stable jobs. The next day, after visiting still more
rallies, Chen uploaded another report to YouTube explaining

22   that "90 percent of the two million" protesters see themselves as peaceful. But there was an active debate about how
the peaceful protesters should perceive the "valiants," the much
smaller group who believed in confrontation and violence. Are
they agitators inviting a more aggressive police response? Or are
they the vanguard, putting their bodies on the line to challenge
the authorities?

On August 20, only three days after he arrived, Chen sud-
denly left Hong Kong. He had come under immense pressure from Chinese officials, concerned by the reach of Chen's
social media posts. The Public Security Bureau had reached out
directly, but more insidious was the indirect pressure campaign.
Officials leaned on Chen's law firm and the lawyers association,
which warned Chen that if he did not return home right away he
would be in grave danger.

Chen flew back to Beijing, mostly because of concerns that
others, including his managers at the law firm, could face consequences as a result of his actions. But there were also consequences for Chen. After he returned from Hong Kong, all his
Chinese social media accounts, including Weibo, WeChat, and
TikTok, were deleted. His ability to open a new account was
thwarted by TikTok's sophisticated facial recognition algo-
rithm, which immediately recognized Chen and deleted his
profile.

Still he did not regret his decision to cover the Hong Kong
protests firsthand. While attending the Hong Kong rallies he
encountered journalists from nearly every major nation—but
not from the Chinese media. He felt he had really contributed
to public understanding through his reporting. He had also
acquired the reporting bug, a desire to know more, dig deeper,

talk to more people, obsessively collect information, and listen
to different perspectives and experiences.

"I came here to foster the communication between the two sides," Chen explained in his last dispatch from the ground in Hong Kong. "I don't want to see disputes or violence by asymmetric information and understanding." After his return from Hong Kong, Chen was interrogated by Chinese police officers who kept asking about his point of view. "No one cares about the truth, all they care about is my stance," Chen observed. "This is the problem we face right now. Truth does not matter at all."

Six months later, on January 23, 2020, the city of Wuhan went into lockdown. The next day, Chen boarded a train from Beijing to Wuhan. He packed his sleeping bag and backpack, expecting to hike the last miles to Wuhan city center. There would be no turning back.

At 10:00 p.m., soon after arriving, Chen uploaded a YouTube video of himself once again speaking to the camera, the imposing Hankou train station's arched central hall flanked by two red-roofed clock towers carefully framed in the background. Clean shaven, his T-shirt replaced with a turtleneck and thick black down jacket, Chen speaks with a kind of manic passion, and the words once again pour out. "Why am I here?" he asks. "It is my responsibility as a citizen journalist. When disaster happens, if you don't rush to the front lines, what kind of journalist are you?"

On December 10, about six weeks before Chen arrived in Wuhan, Wei Guixian, a shrimp seller at the Huanan market, started feeling ill. She went to a local clinic. Eight days later, she was in

24   a hospital fighting for her life. Over the next few weeks, dozens of other Wuhan residents fell ill, many of them connected to the market, which sold fish, meat, and live animals. The vendors on either side of Wei's stall both got sick. In mid-January, Wuhan doctors acknowledged a "cluster of pneumonia cases with an unknown cause." By the end of January, Wuhan health officials had determined that a new coronavirus was spreading through the city.

As doctors and medical personnel began to sound the alarm, local officials in Wuhan worked to cover up the outbreak. When Ai Fen, a director at the Wuhan Central Hospital, posted information on the Chinese social media platform WeChat about the outbreak, she was reprimanded and told not to spread information that could alarm the public. Ophthalmologist Li Wenliang also raised concerns on WeChat about a SARS-like virus. He was immediately questioned by local officials. Chinese censors banned keywords related to the outbreak. At least eight other doctors were questioned. China's National Health Commission ordered institutions "not to publish any information related to the unknown disease" and to "transfer any samples they had to designated testing institutions, or destroy them."

Even as the outbreak began to overwhelm hospitals and medical facilities in Wuhan; even as new cases began to emerge outside China, in Thailand and South Korea; Chinese officials continued to obfuscate, lie, and suppress essential information. They lied about the number of new cases in Wuhan; they told the World Health Organization they had found no clear evidence of human-to-human transmission despite the experience of Wuhan doctors; they directed the Chinese media to downplay or cover up the outbreak. They blocked an international investigation into the origins of the disease and brooked no questions about the presence of viral research labs in Wuhan, even as questions lingered about how the virus, which emerged in bats, had jumped the species barrier to humans (bats were not sold in the Huanan market).

Chen believed fervently that this censorship had facilitated the spread of the disease, and while he was taking every precaution to protect himself against the virus, he was willing to die for the truth. "As long as information travels faster than the virus, we can win this battle," Chen proclaimed. He also threw down the gauntlet. "I don't care where Xi Jinping is," Chen noted, addressing the people of Wuhan. "But I, Chen Qiushi, am here."

Chen's mission to document the truth and share it with China and the world was stymied by the efforts of Chinese censors, who sought to control the reach and influence of his social media. For years, Chen had managed to maintain his voice, through a series of cat-and-mouse maneuvers. But the stakes were about to get a lot higher.

China is often classified as one of the most censored countries in the world, and while that is true, it's much too simple a description. Chinese citizens have access to a broad range of entertainment, news, and information online. Most are either ignorant or indifferent to their government's efforts at control. Ultimately, the goal of the Chinese leadership is not strictly to suppress information. Rather, it seeks to manage it effectively in order to achieve a variety of different objectives. The vision was most fully articulated in an April 2010 presentation by Wang Chen, then deputy director of the Chinese Communist Party's (CCP) Propaganda Department. Wang's speech, which

26   was inadvertently made public, laid out a sweeping and complex vision of the Chinese information environment. China has embraced information technologies, including those that tie it to the world, recognizing that such connections are essential to global economic integration. The leadership also recognized the ways in which the internet can put information at the service of the state, or as Wang put it, open up and broaden "the channels that connect the Party and our government with the masses."

The global information environment, Wang argued, was less advantageous to China's interests. International media like the BBC and CNN dominate the global information space and have a strong anti-China bias that China must fight to overcome. US-based technology companies effectively manage the internet, creating an information hegemony that favors Western notions of free expression and individual liberty rather than the legitimate interest of sovereign states in preserving social harmony.

President Xi Jinping, who assumed leadership in 2013, three years after Wang's speech, has updated and modified these overarching principles, in line with his more authoritarian and centralized approach to governance. That has meant jettisoning any commitment to the media's watchdog role and strengthening the systems that the Chinese government uses to manage and control media coverage. These range from missives and informal contacts to social management. Xi has also made massive investments in China's global propaganda network.

While mass media has been the primary focus, the Xi government has worked to control individual expression and dissent. China has developed and deployed an alternative system of social media centered around multifaceted platforms such as WeChat. In a country as vast and varied as China, it would be

impossible to control and manage individual speech, and this
is not the goal of the Chinese government. It uses keywords,
surveillance, and counter-speech to drown out and minimize
the spread of certain kinds of information it deems as harmful.
But its focus is on rooting out any form of political organizing
online, and it particularly fears "mass movements" of the kind
that compelled pro-democracy activists to take to the streets in
Hong Kong.

This means while there are clear redlines, there is plenty
of critical speech on the Chinese internet. People in China
use WeChat to connect to Chinese-speaking users around the
world, and the platform is a one-stop shop, with integrated cash
transfer capabilities. While China banned the use of uncertified
Virtual Private Networks (VPNs) in 2018, some still use them to
access global social media platforms such as Twitter and You-
Tube, which are officially blocked inside the country. China is
the world's leading jailer of journalists, with forty-seven journalists imprisoned at the end of 2020. That number is alarming,
but given the size of China's population and the robust online
environment, it's equally clear that jailing critics is a last resort.
China prefers to manage speech through the many other, less
visible, means it employs.

China's information management strategies are expen-
sive, requiring a considerable investment in surveillance, monitoring, and media infrastructure. China's goal is to solve a
problem that has bedeviled the modern authoritarian state:
to calibrate the right amount of censorship. Too much means
exclusion from the information economy and disadvantages
the transnational businesses that require modern communications to operate. Too little creates an unacceptable political

28   risk, because technology can propel information and ideas rapidly through society. China believes it has found a perfect equilibrium.

As a lawyer, Chen Qiushi understood the system and was determined to mount his challenge within the law. Yet he was deeply critical of the underlying framework for China's information management, namely that the party was the vanguard of the people and should decide what they know and manage what they think. Chen had a more expansive view of the rights and responsibilities of Chinese citizens, and thought that he could break through the system of information control using his skills as an orator and reporter and his charisma and charm to build an audience.

But as he headed to Wuhan, he was already at a severe disadvantage. His Chinese social media accounts had been deleted and Chen knew that his movements and posts were being monitored. His colleagues in the legal community and at his law firm had passed on warnings from the Chinese authorities that official patience was wearing thin. But Chen also believed in persistence, and in the Chinese Constitution, which declares free expression to be a basic right.

Speaking from the Wuhan train station, Chen acknowledged the challenge. "Although I was blocked on the internet in China for reporting on the events in Hong Kong, I still have a Twitter and YouTube account," he explained. "I invite you to find me through these channels. I'd be happy to help get the voice of the people of Wuhan to the outside world."

Over the next ten days, Chen wandered the suffering city, visiting emergency rooms and supermarkets, talking to doctors, nurses, and ordinary people, and uploading video reports each day. On January 25, the beginning of the Chinese New Year, Chen donned improvised personal protective gear, including swim goggles, to film a chaotic scene outside an emergency room. He also visited the shuttered wet market—which he described as a colorful place that sold foxes, monkeys, and pangolins and "where rich people do have a habit of eating wild animals for health reasons." Chen tried to organize donations of supplies and helped distribute food to hospital workers. He even shared an encouraging note from his parents, who urged him to keep reporting but also to stay safe.

On January 28, Chen visited the site of the Huoshenshan hospital, an enormous emergency facility that the Chinese government was building overnight. The hospital, which was raised from the ground in ten days, was both a response to the overwhelming demand for patient care and a carefully calibrated propaganda effort intended to highlight the ways in which the Chinese system could mobilize state resources and reorganize society in an emergency. Chen, sharing a car ride home to his hotel with several Wuhan residents, filmed the empty streets as he searched for a place to eat, finally locating a lonely restaurant open for takeout.

As the days wore on, Chen became increasingly animated, agitated, and even reckless. On January 30, he uploaded a twenty-seven-minute monologue, in which he decried the shortages of testing kits and hospital beds, described doctors and construction workers collapsing from exhaustion, and reported that taxi drivers in the city had figured out that a contagious disease was spreading in late December, weeks before the authorities made an announcement. (They knew to avoid

30   the Huanan market.) Chen described the growing mayhem at hospitals, the long lines, the patients being treated in parking lots and waiting rooms, and the body of an expired patient unclaimed in a wheelchair.

He bemoaned the Chinese journalists he encountered from state media who, while outfitted in proper protection gear, were unable or perhaps unwilling to cover the news. Equipped with only a cell phone and relying on his wits, Chen was doing the job of the professionals. "Before I came here, no one dared to go to the front line," he complained.

But authorities were closing in. Someone from the Justice Ministry called his phone and asked where he was staying in Wuhan. The Public Security Bureau also phoned. Authorities summoned Chen's parents and asked them to pressure Chen to leave Wuhan. "I want him to return home more than you do," Chen's mother retorted.

Sitting in a spartan hotel room in a white undershirt, his hair rumpled, and his face etched with fear, Chen struck a desperate figure. "I am scared," he acknowledged. "Ahead of me is the virus and behind me the power of law and execution. But I will not back up. As long as I am still alive, I will continue my reporting."

On February 6, Chen told his parents he was planning to visit a temporary hospital. It was his final message. After being unable to reach Chen for twelve hours, his friends, following an agreed-upon protocol, logged on to his account and changed his passwords. Though there was no official confirmation, nearly all suspected he had been detained by Chinese authorities and was being held secretly.

Chen was not the only blogger or citizen to document the hellscape that Wuhan had become. An award-winning Wuhan writer, Wang Fang, who went by the pen name Fang Fang, published a detailed diary of her daily life under lockdown, which became a national and international sensation. The artist and activist Ai Weiwei assembled a powerful documentary from the amateur footage of Wuhan residents, which he titled *Coronation*. It offered a vivid and intimate portrait of doctors on the front lines.

Chen was not even the only blogger to be detained. Several other bloggers and citizen journalists were arrested, including Fang Bin, a Wuhan clothing salesman turned information activist, who filmed dead bodies in a van outside a hospital, and Li Zehua, who traveled from Beijing to Wuhan on February 11 following Chen's disappearance. Li lasted fifteen days in Wuhan, posting a widely viewed report on the shortage of crematorium workers, before being detained on February 26. He reappeared two months later, saying he had been forcibly quarantined, but also praising the police who, he said, "acted in a civilized manner" and "cared about me very much." Another blogger, Zhang Zhan, was not so lucky. In September 2020, four months after her arrest, she was indicted for "picking quarrels and stirring up trouble," a catch-all offense used to snag dissidents. She faced five years in prison.

For a brief period from January to March, Chinese bloggers and journalists had operated in a void, a netherworld in which angry citizens spoke up and shared their grievances. This is a characteristic of the Chinese information space, and after the 2008 Sichuan earthquake and the 2011 high-speed train crash

32 in Wenzhou, there was an outpouring of online criticism before the state could reorganize and respond. While some international media reports described the reporting from Wuhan as an unprecedented challenge to the Chinese government's information hegemony, in hindsight it was just a brief rupture. (Most of the critical reports were circulated on YouTube and Twitter, which is blocked in China, so while they captivated people around the world it's not clear how many people even viewed them in China.) As had happened in the past, the information management system that China has created—a form of just-in-time censorship—was temporarily overwhelmed. But as the Chinese government began to assert greater authority over Wuhan's physical space, and to claim intrusive authority over people's personal lives, it also sought to reorder the information space, and to remove the disruptions.

On March 10, President Xi, who had kept a low profile during the outbreak, delegating day-to-day responsibilities to other officials, visited Wuhan to bolster the spirits of those who made sacrifices in the People's War against the coronavirus. He traveled with hundreds of state journalists, who described how the draconian lockdown in Wuhan, and the extraordinary state mobilization that had kept the population fed and housed, had contained the virus. The government even rehabilitated Li Wenliang, the ophthalmologist whose death from COVID-19 after authorities suppressed his warnings fueled a national outpouring of grief.

Through its global propaganda networks, China began to tell its own story. It used crude measures—a cheesy video distributed by the state-run news agency Xinhua featuring the Statue of Liberty ineptly defending the US virus response—and more sophisticated strategies, like generating media coverage of Chinese dignitaries delivering aid in places like Pakistan and Italy. Part of the government's argument was about the effectiveness of China's system of information control and management, which, it asserted, suppressed misinformation and rumors, while providing the population with necessary health information and protocols to stay safe. A survey released in June 2020 found that 60 percent of people globally believed China had responded effectively to the pandemic, while only one-third felt that way about the US response.

Based on the formula articulated by Wang Chen in his 2010 speech, China's response to the coronavirus outbreak had been a smashing success. The government had used its control over the domestic media—as well as social media—to manage the public response to the coronavirus outbreak and build popular support for its actions. It had isolated domestic dissent, through media management and online blocking and takedowns mostly, while relying on arrests and legal prosecutions in some instances. It had used its propaganda to shape international perceptions and seized the political moment—a time when the world was distracted fighting the pandemic—to move against the independent Hong Kong media, which Chen Qiushi had so admired. It had taken advantage of deteriorating relations with the US and a visa war initiated by the US side to expel more than a dozen US foreign correspondents, many of whom were poking around Wuhan and asking uncomfortable questions. "What the Chinese government wants to tell is a story of triumph," noted Paul Mozur, a longtime *New York Times* reporter and one of those expelled. "They've emerged from the virus as the rest of the world is under siege and under lockdown. And the

34   story they want to tell is that the reason they were able to beat
the virus is the superiority of the Chinese system."

Chen Qiushi's argument that "only freedom of expression
and the freedom of press can protect a country from descending
into a place where the weak are preyed upon by the strong"
was never going to get a hearing. Chen's view, expressed when
he began reporting from Hong Kong, that the Chinese people
deserve the truth, seemed quaint. In fact, because of Chinese
censorship, the truth has become unknowable. We may never
know if the initial cover-up delayed a more systematic response
that could have contained the virus more effectively before it
overran Wuhan and spread to the world. We may never know if
more and complete information would have prompted countries
around the world to recognize the threat earlier and take more
aggressive action, saving millions of lives. We may never know
how the virus first emerged, whether it was naturally occurring
or the result of a lab leak. We may never know whether the censorship that China imposed on Wuhan was simply reflexive, or
the result of something more sinister, an effort to hide China's
negligence or cover up its responsibility.

That possibility is particularly chilling because of the tra-
jectory of repression that followed the disease as it spread
throughout the world. The global crackdown was fueled in
most instances by domestic considerations, as we shall see in
the next chapter, based on a desire to suppress the extent of the
outbreak and its spread and hide government incompetence.
But it was facilitated by a narrative, created by China and promulgated through its propaganda networks, that authoritarian
governments were better equipped to respond to the virus outbreak in part because of their ability to control and manage

information. This was in sharp contrast to the deficiencies in   35
the democratic world, particularly in the United States, and the
failure of the Trump administration, mired in its dysfunction,
to make the case that an open and free society could battle the
disease effectively.

As Wang Chen made clear in his 2010 speech, Chinese censorship is not reflexive, but part of a broader strategic vision of
how information can be utilized to advance the interests of the
state. In a domestic context, limited dissent can be tolerated,
until it creates the risk of political action. This is the framework
that determined Chen's fate. For seven months following his
February 6 disappearance, there was no word regarding Chen's
whereabouts, only rumors that he had been forcibly quarantined. Then in September, Chen's friend, the mixed martial
artist Xu Xiaodong, announced via video that Chen was "in good
health" but living under the supervision of a "certain government department." It was not clear if Chen was in some detention facility, or at home with his parents under the government's
watchful eyes. Chen would not face prosecution, Xu indicated,
but this only made his continued lack of freedom more unjust.
Chen, as a lawyer who assiduously sought to express his dissent
within the confines of the law, was being denied the basic ele-
ments of due process. For the Chinese government, none of this
mattered. What mattered was that Chen, a man who would not
stop talking, had finally been silenced.

The Authoritarian Playbook

The speed with which the pandemic slipped out of China caught autocrats off guard. They feared their rickety public health systems would collapse and that the resulting anxiety and anger would morph into political unrest. So they focused the power of the state on censoring news of the virus rather than the virus itself.

The response to the emerging public health disaster was to deny, dismiss, demean, and detain. If denial, the first tactic, didn't work, authoritarians moved on to the second. States with complex security and religious power structures like Iran, or strong and intolerant militaries like Egypt, used all four.

Autocrats had well-provisioned military and police forces to neutralize physical threats, but combating an unseen enemy like COVID required a different army. Years of underinvestment in public health now made seemingly strong governments vulnerable. They lacked doctors, medical staff, hospitals, and clinics. And they had nothing like the pervasive social control mechanisms of a sophisticated surveillance-state like China to enforce the kind of quarantine imposed on Wuhan.

So, they lied. They lied about the scale of the outbreak, and   37
they lied about their woefully inadequate responses to it. They
got away with this initially because of the nature of the malady
itself. The novel coronavirus could be dismissed as yet another
strain of seasonal flu.

They denied COVID-19 was a problem and cited bogus
infection statistics to prove it, sometimes underreporting
cases by a factor of ten; if questions persisted, they dismissed
the virus and deflected criticism by pointing to the shambolic
response of rich Western countries like the United States as
evidence that they weren't doing so badly after all.

When skeptics including medical staff doggedly challenged those attempted explanations, dictators demeaned
them, undermined their credibility, and forced them to publicly retract their criticism. And when all else failed, there was
always the threat of detention in a COVID-19-infected prison to
silence critics and truth-tellers.

Amid the fear and chaos of the plague, autocrats also sniffed
political opportunity. Under cover of COVID they slipped in
new restrictions on free speech and political expression dressed
up as public health and safety measures. Public gatherings and
demonstrations were banned. Information on the virus that did
not come from the government was criminalized as "fake news"
or propaganda. These censorship measures were justified as
necessary and temporary. It soon became clear, however, that
they were neither.

The ground for such repression was already fertile.
COVID-19 amplified and accelerated a trend toward authoritarianism that the US watchdog Freedom House said had
been underway for the past fifteen years. At least 91 of the 192

38   countries it monitored restricted the news media in response to
       the virus outbreak in the first months of 2020, and 67 percent
       of the states it classifies as "not free" hurriedly introduced new
       curbs on free speech and criticism of the government. For much
       of the world, by the start of 2020, the coming disease was about
       to threaten much more than their health.

       This chapter chronicles four countries that under the cover
       of COVID opportunistically rolled back the positive freedoms
       of citizens to seek and publish information—Russia, Nic-
       aragua, Iran, and Egypt. The leaders of all four have little in
       common, other than a commitment to stamp out dissent. All
       found COVID to be a threat less to the public health than to the
       political order. All four targeted journalists and other indepen-
       dent voices that challenged the official narrative, that COVID
       was a "little flu"; that the government was firmly in charge; and
       that the ravages of the disease in other parts of the world were a
       function of incompetent leadership or the inherent weakness of
       the democratic system.

Russia

The prospect of plague rattled Russia's strongman.

       President Vladimir Putin, who spent much of the early days
       of the pandemic in strict isolation outside of Moscow, delegated
       responsibility for handling the crisis to local and regional offi-
       cials. It was as if he was afraid of being tainted by the virus phys-
       ically and politically. He emerged for a photo-op at a Moscow
       hospital on March 24 in a bright yellow hazmat suit then
       retreated again to his bubble only to discover later that a doctor
       whose hand he had shaken had tested positive for COVID-19. In
       this war, Putin was not going to lead Russia, bare-chested and

on horseback, in a charge against an unseen enemy that exposed
the deep fissures in the economic and social structures that he
had presided over for twenty years.

In an attempt to project competence, Putin dispatched
medical staff and supplies not to Russia's underserved regions
but to northern Italy, then the epicenter of the pandemic in
Europe. He seemed more concerned about burnishing his international image than dirtying his hands at home with a messy
health crisis.

He heaped praise on doctors and nurses but ignored their
warnings and pleas for resources. He promised them bonuses,
which some complained were never fully paid out. Medical staff,
however, did find a voice through social media and independent reporters to expose incompetence, equipment shortages,
and lies. The Kremlin moved quickly to silence them. In March,
media regulator Roskomnadzor ordered the removal of "inaccurate, socially significant information" from some twenty online
media sites. On March 20, it told liberal radio station Ekho
Moskvy to remove an interview with an expert who compared
Putin's handling of COVID-19 with the Soviet Union's bungling
of the 1986 Chernobyl nuclear disaster. The government already
had the power to declare reporting it did not like "fake news"
and levy fines on reporters but that was not enough. On March
31, lawmakers passed amendments to Article 207 of the Criminal Code, which introduced prison terms of up to five years for
spreading "false information." Putin signed them into law the
next day.

Reports about the numbers of infections, deaths, and the
lack of personal protective equipment were top of the censors' list. They seized on a small number of journalists to set an

40   example to others. Police accused Tatyana Voltskaya, a reporter
with the US Congress—funded broadcaster Radio Free Europe/
Radio Liberty in St. Petersburg, of spreading false news over an
April 11 report about supply shortages.

In the central city of Ufa, the editor of the news site *ProUfu*
was fined for reporting on the digging of a thousand graves for
possible COVID-19 victims.

Putin's appointed leader in Chechnya, Ramzan Kadyrov,
expressed his displeasure with COVID-19 coverage in the most
ominous way. On April 13, Kadyrov accused reporter Elena
Milashina of writing "nonsense" and blamed the Federal Security Service for not silencing her. Milashina wrote in the independent newspaper *Novaya Gazeta* that quarantined Chechens
had stopped reporting coronavirus symptoms for fear of being
labeled "terrorists." She said she was "really afraid, as Kadyrov's
threats are really serious and he is a dangerous man. I know that
if he really decides to kill me, he will do it." She reported the
threat to the prosecutor general's office but got no answer. "The
state does not want to defend me," she said.

Much of the media merely amplified the Kremlin's COVID
message. But a handful of journalists persevered in bringing
the public the truth despite threats and prosecutions. *Novaya
Gazeta* ran a series of interviews in late April with hospital staff
and ambulance crews that gave the lie to the official figures on
infections and deaths. As in other authoritarian countries, Russian officials were undercounting infections and attributing
COVID-19 deaths to other causes.

Dmitry Belyakov, a paramedic in the city of Zheleznodorozhny near Moscow, called the figures deceptive and accused
the authorities of fudging the death toll. "I don't believe the

official figures. If a person tests positive for coronavirus but dies
of heart failure, what did they die from? It can be recorded as
either. All our data gathering is built on this [flawed] principle,"
he told the newspaper.

The repression, lies, and incompetence pushed an already
deeply skeptical population into even deeper levels of mistrust.
By July 2020, only 23 percent of Russians said they trusted
Putin, according to a poll by the independent Levada Center. In
an apparent attempt to boost both the economy and his popularity, Putin lifted the few partial lockdowns that had been
imposed and trumpeted Russia's success in keeping its cities
open while western Europe was in an economic coma.

Public mistrust undermined what could have been Putin's
biggest triumph—the rollout of the world's first COVID vaccine. Russia authorized its Sputnik V vaccine in August 2020
after testing on just seventy-nine patients and began admin-
istering it in December. Putin called it "the world's best," but
most Russians ignored it. As a third wave of COVID rolled
across the country from spring 2021, only 16 percent of Russia's 146 million people had been vaccinated. This, coupled
with minimal enforcement of preventative measures, sent the
death rate soaring. Again the government obfuscated the numbers. In the year to March 2021, deaths from COVID reached
97,200, according to official statistics. But the excess mortality
rate tracked by *The Economist* magazine showed excess deaths in
Russia to be a staggering 494,610.

Instead of using health regulations to enforce lockdowns
and mask-wearing, the Kremlin turned them against political
opponents. As protests in support of Putin's political nemesis
Alexei Navalny rocked cities in early 2021, authorities arrested

Navalny's relatives and supporters on charges of violating coronavirus restrictions.

Two events on March 18, 2021, illustrated the Kremlin's cynical political approach. During the day, a Moscow court extended the house arrest of Navalny spokesperson Kira Yarmysh, who had been charged during the protests following Navalny's January arrest with calling on the public to avoid health restrictions. In the evening, Putin sought to boost his sagging popularity by packing more than 80,000 people into the capital's Luzhniki Stadium to mark the seventh anniversary of Russia's seizure of Crimea. Masks were optional. Most people opted not to wear them.

A few months later, Putin took to the international stage to assert that Russia was winning the battle against COVID and recovering economically.

"Our situation is better than in many other countries," he told 5,000 people physically attending the St. Petersburg International Economic Forum in June. "The current situation in Russia and St. Petersburg allows us to hold such events without any particular risk of spreading the infection."

Within a month, daily deaths would reach their highest point of the pandemic. Figures from the Johns Hopkins University Center for Systems Science and Engineering showed that average daily deaths had soared to 670 by mid-July with new daily cases reaching 25,000. The number of daily deaths from a comparable number of infections over the same period in the UK, for example, was 18.

As the failure of the vaccine rollout became apparent, authorities ordered all government workers and service industry employees to get vaccinated. Restaurants and bars in

Moscow could only serve customers indoors if they showed
proof of vaccination. But distrust of the government and its
vaccines runs so deep that the latest push for immunization
has spawned a thriving black market in forged vaccination certificates. Sputnik V, which is similar to the vaccines produced
by AstraZeneca and Johnson and Johnson, could save lives. But
after being lied to for so long, most Russians didn't believe it.

Nicaragua

Unlike Vladimir Putin, Nicaragua's president, Daniel Ortega,
has no pretense to global leadership. At this stage, he just wants
to keep control of his country. But like Putin, Ortega saw COVID
as a threat. A disease is hard to fight with the kind of ideological
bluster that Ortega routinely employs.

Denial and deflection took on a surreal quality when Ortega
disappeared without explanation. As the virus took hold in the
Americas, Ortega was mysteriously out of sight for thirty-four
days, leaving the running of the country to his vice president,
Rosario Murillo, who also happens to be his wife. She may have
been present in body, but her mind floated into a magical realm
worthy of the novels of Gabriel García Márquez. Far from implementing WHO recommendations of lockdowns and social distancing, Murillo called on people to gather and march through
the streets under the slogan "Love in the Time of COVID-19," a
chilling allusion to Márquez's story of a cholera epidemic.

When Ortega resurfaced on April 15, he painted a picture of
a caring and competent government that any Nicaraguan could
see was pure fiction. Nicaragua had no coronavirus problem,
and it was complying with international health recommendations, he boasted. Health care workers were going door-to-door

44   educating households on how to protect themselves from the virus, he asserted without evidence.

He ignored concerns voiced by his Central American neighbors that Nicaragua was becoming a hot zone of infection for the region. He deflected attention away from his handling of the pandemic to that of the United States, which had imposed economic sanctions on Nicaragua after the bloody suppression of anti-government protests in 2018. He said the botched response of the US and Western countries to the disease showed they should invest more in health care than armaments.

As of May 5, the Ministry of Health reported only fifteen confirmed cases, sixteen suspected cases, and five deaths from COVID. A non-government watchdog, the Citizen Observatory for COVID-19, began tracking infections by collating front-line citizen reports. It put the numbers on May 6 at 781 recorded cases of COVID-19, and even that figure was probably too low. By the end of May, the Observatory estimated infections had soared to more than 5,000 and that the dead were being buried at night. Some 700 health care workers wrote Ortega demanding action.

"Deaths could have been avoided," the letter said. "The state cannot continue to evade its responsibility over Nicaraguans' health."

Human Rights Watch later reported that ten public health workers who had signed the letter were fired. Once again an autocrat had put his own political survival above the welfare of the people. Coronavirus testing was discouraged, and health workers intimidated into downplaying the numbers of reported infections and deaths. Some were ordered not to wear protective equipment such as masks in order not to worry the public. Nicaraguans were abandoned to their own devices with no

information or just bad information. Some businesses opted to
close of their own accord, and some individuals wore masks. But
for 6 million people, many of whom live in grinding poverty—
Nicaragua is the second poorest country in the hemisphere after
Haiti—the government had refused to implement health measures that would close the economy and undermine its grip on
power. With many ordinary Nicaraguans struggling and the
world distracted, Ortega slipped in a raft of repressive laws to
ensure his political survival beyond the 2021 presidential elections. In October 2020, Congress passed a "foreign agents" law
that prohibited any person or group such as a human rights
non-governmental organization that receives foreign funding
from participating in internal politics. It also approved a cybercrime law criminalizing the online publication of "false" or "distorted" information and allowing for the jailing of journalists.

Then, in December 2020, Ortega hammered the last nail
in the coffin of free and fair elections, with the introduction of
the Law for the Defense of the People's Rights to Independence,
Sovereignty, and Self-Determination for Peace, which bars "trai-
tors" from holding public office. The definition of "traitor" is so
broad that critics see the law as nothing more than a political
ploy by the former Sandinista guerrilla to prevent viable opposition figures from challenging him for power.

In June 2021, Ortega began rounding up more than twenty
political opponents including six presidential hopefuls. Among
the first was opposition leader and presidential candidate Cristiana Chamorro, daughter of Violeta Chamorro who beat Ortega
in a 1990 presidential election. Police raided her home and
accused her of money laundering. She was placed under house
arrest.

46 Amid the political repression, Ortega doubled down on COVID-denialism, rarely mentioning the virus by name and continuing to suppress infection and death statistics.

In May 2021, while other Central American countries, even those with populations smaller than that of Nicaragua, reported COVID deaths in the thousands, the official WHO death toll for Nicaragua was 184.

At an International Workers' Day rally on May 1 in Managua, the seventy-five-year-old leader did mention one virus but not the coronavirus.

"The most terrible virus that has infected our planet is the virus of capitalism," he told a small maskless crowd.

Iran

Iran's commercial links with the West were restricted by US sanctions, but its ties with China, its biggest trading partner, were flourishing. Daily flights from several Chinese cities ferried students, businesspeople, and workers to colleges and construction projects across the Islamic Republic. It's likely the SARS-CoV-2 virus also hitched a ride.

It spread rapidly among the country's 83 million citizens just as the regime sought to shake off an image of weakness and incompetence after a string of political embarrassments. It was no surprise, therefore, that the clerical establishment, including the octogenarian Supreme Leader Ayatollah Ali Khamenei, who controls the security forces, resisted advice from the Health Ministry to take potentially unpopular steps such as locking down cities and curtailing domestic and foreign travel. Instead, they allowed citizens to continue to attend mosques and large gatherings and visit pilgrimage sites, which accelerated the spread. They also mobilized the population to turn out to celebrate the forty-first anniversary of the revolution and vote in parliamentary elections in February 2020. They did this with full knowledge that a pandemic was upon them.

The virus had slipped into a country whose political and economic immune system was already severely compromised by pervasive censorship and its corollaries, cynicism and mistrust of authority. Prisons were full of political activists and journalists who challenged the regime's hold on power and information. Tightened US sanctions, chronic economic mismanagement, corruption, and a collapsing currency made life for many families a constant struggle to provide the bare necessities. Then, in November 2019, the government abruptly ordered a 50 percent hike in gasoline prices and introduced rationing. The rise pushed a long-suffering population over the edge. Protests erupted in an estimated 70 percent of the country. The Islamic Revolutionary Guards Corps (IRGC), a military force, were dispatched to deal with a civilian protest. They shot dead at least 180 protesters, rounded up others, and shut down the internet to stop news from spreading. The protests proved to be the most widespread political unrest in the Republic's history.

The ruling elites, from Khamenei down through President Hassan Rouhani, the Guards, and the clergy, wanted to show they were in control and enjoyed popular support despite appearances to the contrary. This desire would prove dangerous and even fatal for many Iranians.

Their first move was to deny that COVID-19 was a problem and to discredit or detain those who said otherwise. Social media and messaging apps such as Telegram were abuzz with reports and rumors of infections in January across many regions

48   including the holy city of Qom, a renowned center of religious
study with a world-famous Shia shrine, which attracts pilgrims
from across Iran and beyond. The last thing the administration
wanted was pictures of shuttered holy places and turned-away
pilgrims proving it had failed to contain the pandemic.

Qom is a bastion of the Ayatollahs and the IRGC who
spurned lockdown and social-distancing directives from the
Health Ministry in Tehran that interfered with religious obser-
vance. One practice that went on for weeks as Qom became the
epicenter of the outbreak was the kissing and licking of the sil-
very metal lattice that surrounded the Fatima Masumeh shrine
in the city. It was not until an Instagram post of one of the
"holy-shrine-licker" went viral in early March that the authorities detained one person for violating health regulations. Qom
and other pilgrimage cities like Mashhad remained open to the
thousands who flocked there daily throughout the pandemic.
The authorities dared not close off the cities, but on March 16
they did shut the Masumeh shrine in Qom and the Imam Reza
shrine in Mashhad. This incensed some residents in both cities
and small groups stormed the courtyards of both sites in protest. Qom was also home to thousands of foreign students
and the site of three major Chinese-backed projects, a solar
power plant, a monorail, and the Tehran–Qom–Isfahan High
Speed Rail. The civilian government announced the suspension of flights to and from China on January 31, but a private
Tehran-based airline, Mahan Air, ignored this and carried out
thirty-four flights to and from China between February 1 and
March 5, the news website Sharq revealed.

In February, social media posts about deaths and infections brought a torrent of official denials, but many Iranians just

didn't believe them. Just a month earlier, authorities had denied for days that they had shot down a Ukrainian civilian aircraft leaving Tehran airport on January 8 despite mounting international evidence to the contrary. The IRGC belatedly acknowledged they had accidentally brought down the plane, mistaking it for a missile. They blamed tensions with the United States, which had just assassinated Quds Force commander Gen. Qasem Soleimani in a drone strike in Iraq. The government has banned satellite dishes, blocked websites, outlawed internet censorship circumvention tools, jailed journalists, and spied on and trolled critics. It has banned Twitter, Facebook, YouTube, and Telegram. Despite all this, with the aid of VPNs, many Iranians manage to get news from sources other than the government.

The regime was playing for time ahead of two events where it needed to claim strong public backing. It wanted huge crowds in the street on February 11 to celebrate the anniversary of the 1979 overthrow of the Shah. It also sought a heavy turnout in elections for the Majlis, or parliament, on February 21. It boasted that millions took part in both events, but activists claimed lower turnout figures. They uploaded videos to social media showing anti-government protests on both dates in many cities except in Qom. Turnout for the parliamentary election was the lowest in the Republic's history.

The Iranian government was one of the first to confront one of the confounding paradoxes of the strange disease. Unlike other pandemic diseases—smallpox, the bubonic plague, or even the 1918 Spanish flu whose symptoms were quickly evident—COVID-19 could be hidden in plain sight. The symptoms often resembled those of a common flu, and because the

50   disease tended to strike hardest at the elderly and infirm, severe illness or even deaths were less likely to generate alarm or public attention. The clearest signals that something was awry were overwhelmed hospitals, and if a government could cover that up and withhold testing then it would be possible to pretend that the pandemic was not happening or at the very least was contained. That's what Iran—and so many other countries—did.

With the Majlis election safely behind it, the regime belatedly established a COVID-19 task force to battle a disease that President Hassan Rouhani claimed was a foreign conspiracy. On February 25, Rouhani said that reports about the coronavirus being out of control in Iran was "one of the enemy's plots to bring our country into closure by spreading panic." Other officials similarly blamed the pandemic on the United States.

In an attempt to stem the tide of posts about dissent and COVID-19, the authorities began a counterwave of arrests of those with social media accounts. On February 26, Vahid Majid, commander of the Iranian Cyber Police (FATA), announced dozens of arrests and warned that police were monitoring all online activity to eradicate "misinformation" about the virus. On the same day, the Majlis announced that anyone spreading COVID-19 rumors could be imprisoned for up to three years and flogged. It was the individual courage of medical workers that broke the information blockade.

In an Instagram post on February 3, physician Mostafa Jalalifakhr spoke about how worried he and medical colleagues were about the virus. He said he knew of at least one COVID-19 patient who was in quarantine in the city of Isfahan. The government did nothing. In a February 21 post, Jalalifakhr lamented that time was running out to contain community spread and urged the government to act; he called out the failure to lock down Qom and the northern city of Rasht.

In an attempt to avoid provoking the authorities, the doctor pleaded with readers not to leave "political" comments on his posts. The government can hold those who post stories liable for readers' critical comments. The tactic appeared to have worked and the doctor was not arrested.

Other health care workers were not so lucky. A nurse at Qom's Kamkar Hospital posted a video journal on February 25 to tell Iranians what was happening in the city that was not being covered by official media.

"Last night we lost eight people in one shift, eight of our compatriots; one of them was a twenty-three-year-old woman who had no underlying diseases. Another was a twenty-nine-year-old male, a thirty-year-old man, and a fifty-year-old woman who was talking with me an hour ago and telling me she doesn't understand why her condition is worsening. . . . How long are officials going to make light of this situation?" the nurse asked.

More than two weeks later, on March 9, officials revealed that the nurse, who was not named, had been arrested. It was the first time that the authorities had acknowledged arresting medical personnel.

Defying intimidation and censorship, Iranians circulated news of infections and deaths and lambasted the authorities. The pressure to acknowledge that Qom was in the grip of the virus finally became too great. On February 18, Health Ministry officials confirmed that COVID-19 was spreading through the holy city. Mohammad Reza Qadir, head of Qom University of

52   Medical Sciences, who had denied reports about the spread in the city just one day earlier, finally confirmed that two patients had died from the virus.

The authorities then pivoted to play down the scale of the deaths. On February 24, Qom member of parliament Ahmad Amirabadi Farahani announced that fifty people had died in the city and that he had personally given the names of forty of them to the Health Ministry. Deputy Health Minister Iraj Harirchi said if the toll were even a quarter of that, he would resign on the spot. He did not.

The deputy minister, who was later confirmed to have the virus, then went on television twice to dismiss COVID-19 as no worse than the flu. In the middle of a press conference, he broke out into a fever sweat and was handed a box of tissues to mop his brow. Then in a television studio he sunk his face into the crook of his arm to shield his interviewer from the spray of a coughing fit. The weary skepticism of Iranians toward their political class ran so deep that some even thought Harirchi was faking COVID-19 symptoms so that he could reemerge a few days later to "prove" that the virus was indeed no worse than a bad cold.

It was only as officially reported deaths neared one thousand that the government ordered the shrine in Qom closed on March 16.

The government was now so determined to show the world that it was in control that it rescinded permission for the charity Médecins sans Frontières to set up a fifty-bed COVID treatment unit in the city of Isfahan after two cargo planes with MSF equipment had already landed in Tehran.

Iran's public health care system had handled epidemics successfully in the past, with cholera outbreaks in the 1980s

and SARS in the early 2000s. But this time Khamenei effectively bypassed the Health Ministry by putting the paramil-
itary Basij, a part of the Revolutionary Guard, in charge of
enforcing pandemic countermeasures with little or no training.
Part of their mission in some places was to go door-to-door
checking for infections and distributing pamphlets with
prayers recommended by the Supreme Leader for stopping
COVID-19. They also arrested anyone they deemed to be
spreading propaganda. The result of this militarization of a
health crisis was predictable, according to Amir Afkhami, a
professor of psychiatry, global health, and history at George
Washington University. Many Iranians failed to report infections for fear of government retaliation, adding to the well of
ignorance and depriving epidemiologists of one their most
useful tools, contact-tracing.

Nevertheless, some Iranians wrote social media posts
giving the lie to the government's claims about the pandemic.
Enforcement of the law to prevent distribution of such information was erratic and selective. Some posters were arrested,
others forced to retract their posts.

Even mainstream media sometimes had to row back on stories that got too close to the truth. The semiofficial Iran Labor
News Agency (ILNA) ran a video interview on March 25 with a
nurse from a hospital in Qazvin who said staff had been dealing
with the virus for fifty-one days. Social media pounced on this
as evidence that COVID-19 had been infecting Iranians since
early February, contrary to the Islamic Republic's assertions.

The very next day, ILNA was forced to do a second interview with the same nurse in order to silence those "attempting
to create doubts about when the virus was first identified in the

54   country." The nurse, who was not named, was made to explain that the hospital was treating influenza and other respiratory ailments before COVID-19 emerged and that was why she had not been home for fifty-one days.

Categorizing COVID-19 as anything but COVID-19 became commonplace, according to Dr. Afkhami. Between February and April 2020, the Health Ministry reported 3,400 deaths from coronavirus but 13,300 fatalities and 178,000 hospitalizations from acute respiratory syndrome, he said. In 2019, over the same period, acute respiratory syndrome cases were running at about 4,800 a month, he said. "A lot of these new cases were being called something else when it was clear to the doctors taking care of them they were dealing with coronavirus."

This cover-up undoubtedly cost lives. Iran fared worse than any other country in the Middle East, even acknowledging that death and infection statistics across the region are flawed due to underreporting and lack of testing. By the end of 2020, Iran had recorded some 1.2 million cases and 55,000 deaths—650 deaths per million inhabitants. Its neighbor Iraq saw the next highest toll in the region with 13,000 deaths over the same period, or 315 per million people. And even these figures from Iran might be an underestimate. As early as August 9, Mohammad Reza Mahboobfar, a member of the national coronavirus task force, broke ranks with colleagues to accuse the government of hiding the scale of the tragedy from the Iranian people.

"In my opinion the health ministry figures are one-twentieth of the actual figures," he told *Jahan Sanat* newspaper in an interview. The paper was banned for twenty days by the Press Supervisory Board for carrying the interview with the headline "Do Not Trust Government Statistics."

The government's attempts to downplay COVID-19 and   55
censor information was the fundamental characteristic of its
response. In March 2020, it suspended the distribution of print
newspapers and stepped up the blocking of websites. On April
29, the armed forces announced that 3,600 people had been
arrested for spreading false information about the pandemic.
Censorship and imprisonment may have slowed the spread of
news but not infection. Iran was the epicenter of the pandemic
in Central Asia and the Middle East. But it was not alone in the
region in its failed authoritarian and militarized response to a
public health disaster. Egypt, the most populous Arab country,
was also reading from the authoritarian playbook.

Egypt

Egypt sits at the other end of the geopolitical spectrum from
Iran. It is an ally of the United States, has diplomatic ties with
Israel, relies on US military aid, and welcomes Western tourists as a vital source of income. But like Iran, Egypt militarized its response and sought to play down the virus and censor
reporting about it. Former general Abdel Fattah el-Sisi, whom
President Trump called his "favorite dictator," had been ruthless with political opponents, dissidents, human rights advocates, and the independent press since coming to power after a
2013 military takeover.

COVID-19 provided the cover to continue that repression,
extend a state of emergency, and keep Egypt's already over-
crowded prisons filled with anyone who dared raise a voice
against him.

It proved relatively straightforward at first for officials
to decide what Egyptians learned about the pandemic. The

56 government and its allies controlled most mainstream media, and even the handful of online independent news sites like Mada Masr and al-Manassa that still managed to operate were often blocked, depriving them of readers and revenue. Egypt has blocked some six hundred websites covering news and politics since 2017, according to Human Rights Watch.

Khaled el-Balshy watched the censoring of the pandemic with growing alarm. In March 2020 the veteran journalist resolved to provide Egyptians with facts by launching the online news site Darb (Path). It took just a month for the authorities to block it in Egypt. Unfazed, el-Balshy began posting content on Facebook and other social media, and the site remained viewable abroad. Then, in September 2020, authorities arrested el-Balshy's brother, Kamal, who is not a journalist, in an attempt to get Khaled to stop publishing. He did not.

The foreign media in Egypt had enjoyed a little more latitude in its reporting, but ever since the 2018 expulsion of *Times* of London correspondent Bel Trew, resident Western reporters had felt the government's red lines for reporting were increasingly and deliberately blurred. Ruth Michaelson, *The Guardian*'s Cairo correspondent, knew like many Egyptian journalists in early January that a wave of infection was about to wash over the country and that the government was lying about it. As underequipped hospital wards filled with COVID-19 patients in mid-January, she reported along with the local independent press on a clear lack of medical oxygen to treat them, and on the government's bald denials, despite video footage of untreated patients, that there was an oxygen shortage.

By mid-March, Egypt had reported just 166 infections and 4 deaths in a country of 100 million people. It seemed desperate not to frighten off foreign tourists. Even after an outbreak on a Nile cruise ship in the southern city of Luxor in February, tourist sites had remained open. Tourism employs about one in ten Egyptians.

"I literally built my own spreadsheet to track the number of tourists leaving Egypt and declaring that they were infected, either as a result of being there themselves or in connection with people that were there because there's no way the government would ever put out that data because they view it inherently as a security risk," Michaelson said.

On March 15, Michelson published a story that was to be her last dispatch from Cairo. Epidemiologists at the University of Toronto had modeled the spread of the virus in Egypt on what scant data was available and estimated that between 6,000 and 19,000 Egyptians were infected with the disease. Michaelson picked up their report.

A senior official demanded that either she publish a retraction and an apology or furnish the names of each of the 19,000 cases that she knew had COVID. Her press accreditation was revoked and she left Egypt. The message to the remaining foreign press in Cairo was clear.

The regime could not expel skeptical Egyptian journalists and bloggers, so it resorted to its usual practices, which range from censoring, co-opting, intimidating, and prosecuting, to finally imprisoning them. At least ten were detained in the first months of the pandemic, many for reporting on the disease's impact. A favored censorship tactic was to hold reporters in indefinite pre-trial detention while prosecutors investigated such charges as spreading false news, misusing social media, and joining a terrorist organization.

58   Even before the coronavirus, Egypt's prisons were infamous for their insanitary conditions. In the grip of the pandemic, they became a hot zone of infection that was to cost at least one journalist his life.

"I am very sick. Please do something before I run out of breath," gasped Mohamed Monir.

"I need oxygen therapy," the journalist pleaded in a Facebook Live post from his Cairo home after release from jail. Journalists rallied to his aid but it was too late. On July 13, he died from complications due to COVID-19. He was eulogized by one colleague as a "martyr for press freedom in Egypt."

In order to hide the scale of the outbreak from ordinary citizens, the regime had to discredit or muzzle medical professionals who chose not to remain silent as patients and colleagues died from the virus for lack of adequate resources.

Egypt adopted a dual strategy toward health care providers. It praised them collectively and sanctioned individuals who pointed out problems or failures.

The airwaves hummed with praise for the "white army," an allusion to medical workers' lab coats, on the front lines. State media pumped out stories that showed the administration in command with "statistics" to back it up. Meanwhile, doctors were telling a different story on social media.

Like some of his fellow autocrats, el-Sisi chose to confront a virus as if it were a terrorist threat. He unleashed the feared National Security Agency (NSA), which proceeded to intimidate and arrest medics. On March 28, 2020, a twenty-six-year-old doctor in the Mediterranean port city of Alexandria was picked up and placed in pre-trial detention on the same trio of charges used against the media: spreading false news, misusing social

media, and membership in a terrorist organization. Dr. Alaa
Shaaban Hamida's crime was to allow a nurse to use her phone to
report a case of coronavirus. The director of the El Shatby University Hospital where she worked had reported her for ignoring
his order banning direct communication with the outside.

Egypt's Doctors Syndicate reported a string of detentions
of medical professionals as the virus spread and exposed the
cracks in a creaking health care system that over the years had
received a tiny fraction of the billions of dollars el-Sisi has lav-
ished on the military.

On May 25, a group of doctors at Cairo's al-Mounira hospital resigned in protest at a lack of proper equipment and poor
administration, which they believed contributed to the death
from COVID-19 of their colleague Walid Yehia, thirty-two.
Their action prompted a visit from NSA agents who pressured
them to retract their resignations.

By July, at least eight doctors and two hospital pharmacists
had been detained for revealing the truth, including a Cairo ICU
doctor, Ahmed Safwat, who merely described in a Facebook post
a situation that Egyptians could see for themselves. "The government says that everything is fine and under control, but you
enter hospitals and find the opposite."

The government's inadequate response was literally costing
doctors their lives. By mid-year the reported national death toll
from COVID-19 reached four thousand, about the same as that
of South Africa. The difference, however, was that while six doctors died in South Africa over the same period, Egypt recorded
117 deaths. By the end of 2020, that figure had surpassed 200.

The true scale of the pandemic in Egypt may never be
known. Testing was inadequate in the public sector and private

60   clinics were not systematically passing on test results to the Health Ministry.

With just 140,000 cases and 7,400 deaths by the end of 2020 in a country that introduced only partially enforced lockdowns and social distancing, the official statistics are so low as to be part of the cover-up. In a dictatorship, citizens are not meant to know the truth. Those who refused to remain in ignorance paid with their liberty, or in the case of some doctors and journalists like Mohamed Monir, with their lives.

The censoring of information about the nature of SARS-CoV-2 and its ravages not only needlessly cost lives, but it also turned what could have been just a public health emergency into a global crisis of civil and political rights. Freedom House estimates that 75 percent of the world's population lives in countries that have suffered a deterioration in rights and democracy as a result of the disease. The number of countries it classifies as "not free" has risen to fifty-four from forty-five in the past decade and a half.

Just as we saw leaders like Putin use health restrictions to crack down on political protests, autocrats from Cambodia to Venezuela latched onto the pandemic to suppress political opposition.

COVID pulled back the curtain on the workings of many of these "strongman" regimes as demonstrated by Egypt. Autocracies can be rigid and fragile. The response to this pandemic demanded flexibility and resilience. Regimes like Iran and Egypt that are dependent on military support knew this and felt threatened. After years of being lied to, populations were skeptical. Denial and deflection did not work. So, their rulers

resorted to demeaning medical professionals and detaining   61
anyone who contradicted the official line.

Political leaders used the scarce resources of the state
to suppress information and freedoms rather than combat
the disease. It proved to be a deadly example and precipitated
the greatest single sustained assault on basic civil and political rights since the War on Terror. With democratic countries
overwhelmed managing their own response, and with China
asserting that strong state power was essential to confronting
the pandemic, these authoritarian governments faced little
scrutiny and almost no international pressure to tamp down
their repressive action.

The Democratic Populists

Luiz Henrique Mandetta, Brazil's Minister of Health, was feeling uneasy. In December 2019, when he first heard rumors that a new virus had erupted in Wuhan, China, Mandetta wrote to the World Health Organization to ask for an explanation. None was forthcoming. He closely followed the Chinese response, and while he took some comfort from the fact that the spread of the disease appeared to have been contained, he never trusted the official numbers. When Iran was slammed next, Mandetta struggled to find an explanation. Maybe it was the US embargo, or Iran's collapsing health system, or its theocratic system of government, that had made the country vulnerable. But he couldn't shake the images of the overwhelmed hospitals, of people being buried in mass graves dug by tractors. "We kind of said okay, there is something more about this that is not being explained yet," Mandetta recalled.

But then what happened in Italy—an explosion of new cases that over the course of a few weeks overwhelmed a modern

European health care system—made it impossible to rationalize   63
further. "It was the first democratic country with an open press
that really showed the drama," Mandetta acknowledged. Brazil
needed to take action.

In many autocratic countries, as outlined in the last chapter,
governments used repressive measures to suppress critical
information about the spread of COVID-19 and to cover up
their own incompetence. In some cases, they downplayed the
threat posed by the disease while also usurping new powers
they claimed they needed to fight against it (autocrats are not
generally sticklers for logical consistency).

In populist-led democracies—notably Brazil, the US, and
India, which are the focus of this chapter—leaders relied on
new forms of censorship to achieve a similar result. Since jailing
critics and blocking websites were generally off the table, their
strategy was to attack and undermine independent sources
of information, unleash harassing trolls on their critics, and
spew out misinformation to confuse the public. These systematic attacks on experts and independent institutions, including
medical professionals, the scientific community, and critical
journalists, not only weakened democracy and undermined trust
and accountability, they led to terrible public health outcomes.
This poor performance in turn helped fuel the Chinese narrative, reinforced through Beijing's global propaganda networks,
that authoritarian forms of government were better equipped to
respond to the pandemic. As this perception took hold, it gave
political cover to autocratic leaders amplifying the waves of
repression that took place throughout the world, a vicious cycle
that defined the initial response to the COVID-19 pandemic.

For Mandetta, the immediate challenge was both straightfor-ward and immensely daunting: getting his own government to recognize and acknowledge the gravity of the threat. A medical doctor and orthopedic surgeon from the southwestern state of Mato Grosso do Sul bordering Paraguay, Mandetta served in Congress for eight years as a Democrat, which in Brazil is the conservative party. He was a staunch critic of President Dilma Rousseff of the leftist Workers' Party (PT), including the Mais Medicos program that sent Cuban doctors to work in poor communities. He was a reluctant recruit to the government of President Jair Bolsonaro, at least as he tells the story. Man-detta had left Congress and was moving to his wife's hometown of Rio de Janeiro when the president called him and asked if he would be willing to serve in his administration. "I asked him one question," Mandetta explained. "Is this a technical choice or a political choice?" Mandetta insisted he was not interested in a political appointment.

Bolsonaro assured Mandetta that politics would not be a consideration when it came to the health of Brazilians. Man-detta is a man of formidable political ambitions himself whose name has been mentioned as a possible presidential candi-date. He has not been untouched by allegations of corruption. But Mandetta said he accepted the ministry job with a narrow mandate focused on public health, and assembled several dozen experts to help him carry out his program. "We had a wonderful team," he recalled.

In the first year on the job, Mandetta traveled the world to build relationships with his counterparts in Russia, China, and the United States. He participated in a global campaign focused on the eradication of tuberculosis. In fact, when Mandetta first heard about the outbreak of a new disease in Wuhan he tried to get in touch with the Chinese health minister but never heard back.

Mandetta was deeply frustrated by the lack of response. It was clear to him that China was trying to cover up the outbreak, something he believed would not be possible in a democratic country with a free press. When Mandetta attended the World Economic Forum in Davos, Switzerland, from January 21–24, one of four health ministers to do so, he saw further evidence of Chinese duplicity. Mandetta was supposed to meet on the side-lines with Dr. Tedros Adhanom Ghebreyesus, the head of the World Health Organization. But Tedros canceled his trip. He had to stay in Geneva, he explained, to host a meeting on whether to declare the coronavirus outbreak a global health emergency. The Chinese blocked the declaration, Mandetta alleged, a position that in Mandetta's view undermined the WHO's credibility and showed its subservience to China. "I was talking to the guy from the United States. I was talking with Italy, with Germany, with England," Mandetta recalled. "We were all asking each other what is it all about? What kind of information or inside infor-mation do you have about the disease?"

A month after the Davos meeting, in late February, the first case of COVID-19 was detected in Brazil. It was toward the end of Carnival, and predictably other new infections emerged in the subsequent days. Mandetta tried to raise the alarm. President Bolsonaro and his advisors were not having it. Instead they were focused on their upcoming visit to the United States, where Bolsonaro and his good friend President Trump were planning a get-together at Trump's Mar-a-Lago resort to discuss trade.

66   Mandetta was invited to be part of the presidential entou-
rage, but begged off. "I mean it's just a political trip, not a technical trip," Mandetta reasoned. "There's nothing in Florida for a
health minister to speak about. I'm staying in Brazil."

Indifferent to the looming threat, Presidents Trump and
Bolsonaro gathered with their families and staff for the fes-
tive dinner in Mar-a-Lago on Saturday, March 7. Trump hosted
the dinner outdoors under a yellow-striped tent, but afterward
many guests migrated to the ballroom where a party had been
planned to celebrate the birthday of Kimberly Guilfoyle, girl-
friend to Trump's son Donald Trump Jr. As the evening wore
on, the celebration picked up steam. Glasses were raised and
toasts were offered, including a tribute from Senator Lindsey
Graham who proclaimed that Guilfoyle represented everything
"Bernie Sanders hates." A rousing rendition of "Happy Birthday"
followed, with President Trump joining in. Waiters brought out
a cake with sparklers embedded. Later, the celebrants formed a
conga line, winding their way through the crowd as a disco ball
spun and purple light infused the room.

Mandetta later dubbed Bolsonaro's visit to Mar-a-Lago "a
COVID trip." Seventeen members of the forty-person delegation that traveled to Florida eventually tested positive for coronavirus, Mandetta claimed (Bolsonaro himself contracted the
disease in July). Miami mayor Francis Suarez, who had met with
Bolsonaro, also tested positive as did several guests who had
attended the festivities at the resort.

As concerned as he was about the situation, Mandetta
believed there was a silver lining, which was that having seen
the ravages of the disease President Bolsonaro would need to
take COVID-19 seriously. "It's too close," Mandetta reasoned.

"People are starting to die." But the president was unmoved.
Instead of embracing social distancing, mask-wearing, and
other measures that could help slow the spread of the disease,
Bolsonaro took the opposite tack. As soon as he returned from
the US, Bolsonaro's education minister used racist language
("BLazil") to claim that China was in a conspiracy to use the
virus for "world domination." Later, Bolsonaro himself attacked
China, and began touting the benefits of the antimalarial drug
hydroxychloroquine, claiming that after taking it, "I was 100
percent better. So, it worked for me. I'm the living proof." He
opposed mask-wearing and urged people to get on with their
lives, and keep the economy open. The behavior was so strange
and outlandish that Mandetta thought that Trump had shared
secret information with Bolsonaro about an imminent cure,
something right out of a Hollywood movie. "I figured they are
big friends, and probably know something we don't know."

Mandetta later came to believe instead that Trump and Bolsonaro had coordinated around a political strategy intended to
outrun the disease and deflect blame. Beyond what Mandetta
called the "chaos theories," the lies and disinformation that
provided a scapegoat and gave people false hope, the key pillar
was to play both sides of the street by allowing governors and
mayors to make all the hard decisions and then attacking them
for their incompetence if the virus spread and for overreacting
if it didn't. In Brazil, that strategy got an inadvertent assist from
the Brazilian Supreme Court, which ruled in March 2020 that
the states had the authority to impose restrictions in order to
control the spread of COVID and these restrictions could not
be superseded by the federal government. Bolsonaro took the
Supreme Court decision as a license to do nothing. Like Trump,

68   he pandered to his base by calling for people to get back to work, while avoiding any responsibility for the hundreds of thousands of avoidable deaths.

On February 24, 2020, a few weeks before his dinner with Bolsonaro, President Trump had traveled to India for a two-day visit with his other good friend Prime Minister Narendra Modi. The brief tour, which had been dubbed Namaste Trump, a rejoinder to the Howdy Modi rally that the two presidents' supporters had organized in Houston the previous September, was short on policy but long on the pomp and ceremony that Trump enjoyed. The crowd that came out to greet Trump in Ahmedabad, however, was only a fraction of the 10 million Modi had promised. The massive cricket stadium where the two presidents held a rally was full at the outset, but many, wilting in the blistering heat, left before the remarks were complete. Still, Trump did not hold back, proclaiming, "America loves India. America respects India," and heaping praise on Modi, whom he called "very tough" and a "very tough negotiator."

Despite the fact that the World Health Organization had by then overcome China's resistance and declared COVID-19 a Global Health Emergency, the threat posed by the new disease did not figure prominently on the bilateral agenda. While Mandetta believes that Trump and Bolsonaro coordinated their COVID response strategy at the Mar-a-Lago dinner, there is no evidence of any such direct coordination between Modi and Trump. Instead, the similarities in approach between Trump and Modi stem from a shared outlook and vision as populists who have used the stature and influence conferred by their office to attack and marginalize their critics while undermining the democratic institutions that constrain their power.

Modi had throughout his political career cast himself as a kind of monk-warrior, personally ascetic but ruthless in his efforts to create a dynamic and prosperous India, grounded in Hindu identity. The Indian media has helped drive the narrative, but only a few weeks after Trump's visit it had collided with a rather inconvenient reality: India was seeing a spike in COVID infection. Unlike Trump and Bolsonaro, Modi acknowledged the risk and took action, instituting a nationwide lockdown on March 24. But the lockdown, enacted with only four hours' notice, produced untold hardship and a political backlash, which Modi suppressed through heavy-handed measures that deeply compromised India's democracy.

Most of India's 1.3 billion people live in impoverished conditions despite India's recent economic growth, and the urban workforce is largely composed of rural migrants who survive hand to mouth. The nationwide lockdown left millions of workers, deprived of their income, with no money for food or rent. People also had no way to return to their villages since the transportation network was also shut down. Workers traveled for days on foot or bicycle. Later, some states provided free buses, and special train service was restored, to transport migrant workers home.

The lockdown, which many believed played a role in controlling the spread of COVID during the first wave, allowed the Modi government to set a narrative: bold action from the country's visionary and fearless leader had saved India from calamity. Anyone who challenged this narrative—particularly in the media—was shunned and attacked. Journalists and others who raised concerns about the confusion, the human hardship, the logistical challenges, and the government infighting

70 surrounding the nationwide shutdown faced harsh reprisals. What Modi demanded from the country's media was obeisance; he told top executives in a meeting on March 24 that they should publish positive and inspiring stories and combat "pessimism, negativity, and rumor mongering." Just in case journalists didn't get the message, the Modi government went to the Supreme Court to request an injunction requiring that they report only the official version. It was denied. But his government used regulations and economic pressure to squeeze critical broadcasters. Like Trump and Bolsonaro, Modi relied on an army of online trolls who amplified his criticism of individual journalists, attacking them in the most personal and vile ways, particularly female journalists who were subjected to rape threats and doctored pornographic images. New restrictions were imposed on international journalists, and local reporters faced a wave of violence and repression that included more than ten arrests, according to data compiled by CPJ.

Two days after the lockdown began, two local journalists in the northern state of Uttar Pradesh reported that children were going hungry because families had not acquired food before the lockdown. Local officials responded by filing legal notice against the reporters for publishing false and sensational information. Less than a week later, on April 1, police in the state took legal action against Siddharth Varadarajan, the editor of the online portal The Wire, and one of India's most prominent English-language journalists. Among the charges against him was "spreading rumors with intent to cause a riot." While the Modi government was vilifying Muslims and implying that they were spreading the virus, Siddharth revealed that the Uttar Pradesh chief minister, Yogi Adityanath, a prominent Modi

supporter and member of his Hindu nationalist BJP party, had
participated in a religious ceremony without social distancing a
day after the lockdown was announced.

The press crackdown in India dovetailed with sweeping
restrictions on assembly imposed in the name of fighting
COVID-19 but used to suppress protests by civil activists protesting discrimination against India's Muslim minority. The
shutdown of the court system was used to slow-walk the legal
process against Muslim activists, who were jailed for extended
periods in unsafe conditions.

The nationwide lockdown was an unprecedented restric-
tion on the liberty that Indian citizens enjoy in a democracy.
But it had a public health rationale, and many citizens, including
health experts, believed it was warranted. But the repressive
action taken by Modi to stifle criticism served no other legitimate purpose. These measures, along with many other efforts
taken by the Modi government to consolidate its political project
grounded in Hindu nationalism, caused the democracy watchdog
Freedom House to reclassify India as partly free rather than free,
a devastating assessment for a country that has proudly touted
itself as the world's largest democracy. Moreover, Modi's hubris
over the success of the nationwide lockdown caused him to
lower his guard, lifting nearly all COVID restrictions between
January and April 2021. The shift was in part motivated by a
desire to restart the Indian economy, but it also had a political
logic, which was to allow Modi's BJP party to encourage participation in Hindu religious festivals and to resume campaign rallies for the important state elections in May.

Because the second wave undermined Modi's claims of
success, the government was slow to take action even as the

72   country's health system was overwhelmed. Unable to obtain basic medical supplies, including oxygen, families turned to miracle remedies peddled online, and rumors and misinformation proliferated. The Modi government responded not by seeking to meet the information needs of a society subsumed in crisis, but rather by cracking down on online speech critical of its performance, including tweets calling for the prime minister's resignation. Thousands of COVID-related fatalities were reported each day, but bodies washing up on the shores of the Ganges and mass funeral pyres that lit up the night belied the government data. Journalists who traveled to rural villages to count the dead alleged that the toll may have been five times higher than reported.

Back in Brazil, Mandetta was closely monitoring the way the disease was playing out around the world, particularly in Europe and the United States. On March 8, the morning following the Mar-a-Lago dinner with Trump and Bolsonaro, all of northern Italy went into lockdown. In Bergamo, the healthy barricaded themselves in their homes, becoming some of the first in Europe to experience the full horror of the disease. The crushing sense of isolation and powerlessness caused by confinement was reinforced by the silence of the streets, a silence punctuated by the wails of ambulances transporting the sick to overwhelmed hospitals. Cut off from their loved ones, COVID patients suffered and died alone. They were also buried alone. On March 18, a convoy of thirty-six military trucks evacuated the dead from Bergamo in body bags and coffins for interment in other parts of Italy.

Mandetta also watched the developments in the United   73
States with increasing alarm. Given what he understood as the
possible strategic coordination between Trump and Bolsonaro,
he feared the spread of COVID in the US could be a foretaste
of what Brazil might experience. The feckless response in the
White House increased his sense of foreboding.

By late January, the White House had set up a COVID task
force led by Health and Human Services Secretary Alex Azar,
which was staffed with a seemingly random assortment of
political appointees, according to Olivia Troye, the Homeland
Advisor to Vice President Mike Pence, who participated in the
task force meetings. Many members, according to Troye, used
their positions to push for policies that seemed unrelated to
protecting public health, from shutting down the US-Mexico
border to getting tough with China. The doctors and scientists were sidelined and effectively marginalized, along with the
leadership at the Centers for Disease Control.

In late February, a stark public warning from Senior CDC
official Nancy Messonnier about the inevitability of community
spread caused the US stock market to tank, infuriating Trump,
whose reelection strategy depended on a strong economy. The
president responded by appointing Pence to lead the coronavirus task force, perhaps as a way of projecting seriousness and
calm. Pence himself was completely blindsided by the move,
according to Troye. Since Trump, like Bolsonaro, had delegated
the COVID response to state and local officials, Pence was put in
charge of coordination.

Troye's role was to make sure that the vice president had
the most accurate and timely information in order to make

74   informed decisions. The problem was that the information environment in the White House was utterly chaotic. It went beyond the inevitable confusion created by the crisis itself and struck Troye as a deliberate effort by the president and his acolytes to disrupt and undermine an effective policy discussion. "It was a pandemic of disinformation," Troye recalled. "The credible experts are competing with external voices that are not in the room."

First, Troye struggled to get basic information about what was happening in China, a country that is notoriously a black hole for the intelligence community. Every conversation about the virus's origins was disrupted by wild conspiracy theories generally spouted by Peter Navarro, the Senior Advisor to the President who ostensibly had a trade portfolio and was also known to have Trump's ear. Navarro kept insisting that the virus escaped from a Chinese bioweapons facility. Troye found no evidence to support this contention, but questions about it kept coming up in meetings, including from the vice president.

Navarro, meanwhile, seemed to become more and more unhinged. At one point Navarro alleged in a media interview that Dr. Anthony Fauci had somehow conspired with China to engineer the coronavirus. The effect of the wild accusations made by Navarro and also by President Trump himself was to gum up the policy discussion, creating a kind of paralysis, while also misleading and disorienting the public. The situation became so untenable that on several occasions Troye maneuvered to prevent Navarro from getting in to see the vice president, physically blocking access to Pence's offices while politely offering to relay a message. "Once you've lost credibility you've lost the battle," Troye lamented. "The narrative just kept shifting above our head."

Then there was the bizarre debate over mask-wearing. Marc Short, the vice president's chief of staff, seemed uninterested in battling the disease and would roll his eyes at meetings whenever COVID came up because he saw the disease response as taking time and attention away from Trump's reelection campaign. Short adamantly refused to wear a mask. In the Trump White House, only doctors and medical professionals walked around with face coverings.

The personal views of the anti-maskers were reflected in policies, including efforts by the president and others to undermine commonsense public health initiatives intended to slow the rate of infection, notably a plan for the government to distribute free masks to every American household. There was also an awareness that insisting that Americans wear masks could be politically costly in an election year because, as Troye's White House colleagues reminded her, "Americans really like their freedom. They don't like being told what to do. We're not a mask-wearing society."

While Mandetta was not aware of the dysfunction inside the task force, he was very aware of the absence of federal leadership, which he linked to the terrible COVID surge in New York City. There, New York City's Democratic mayor, Bill de Blasio, and New York State's Democratic governor, Andrew Cuomo, were engaged in an ugly political battle, neither willing, at least initially, to make the tough calls. In early March, with the virus spreading rapidly and cases growing by the day, de Blasio encouraged New Yorkers to maintain their normal lives, to ride the subway, to go out to restaurants. Neither would pull the trigger on closing the schools, even as teachers balked and students stayed home. The delay, experts agreed, cost thousands of lives.

"When I saw New York falling apart, when I saw hospitals being built in Central Park, when I saw people in intensive care units, I noticed that Trump stepped back and gave Fauci the coordination," Mandetta said. (In fact, Fauci did not formally coordinate the government's response, but was in an increasingly visible role during this period.) "I figure that the Brazilian president is going to do the same, but he did not." That was the breaking point for Mandetta. He decided to lead an information insurgency against his own government.

Each day at 5:00 p.m., Mandetta would brief the Brazilian media on the latest developments, speaking for several hours and providing sober, accurate, and timely information about the spread of the disease around the world and the steps that Brazilians needed to take to protect themselves. At first the media was invited to attend in person, but as cases rose Mandetta moved to a remote format, creating a WhatsApp group where journalists could submit questions and receive materials. The briefings were transmitted live on Facebook, Twitter, and YouTube, and information was also shared on Instagram, making Mandetta a media star and raising his profile immensely. Flanked by his advisors and clad in the distinctive blue vest of the Health Ministry, Mandetta advised Brazilians to stay home, wear masks, and wash their hands frequently.

The daily briefings were a direct challenge to President Bolsonaro, who despite his own close call, continued to ignore social-distancing requirements, wading into crowds of supporters and encouraging Brazilians to get on with their normal lives. The president spewed lies and disinformation about the disease and supposed cures, relentlessly attacking his critics on social media, goading the online mob to hurl the most vicious

abuse, a tactic that Brazilian journalist Patrícia Campos Mello
dubbed the "hate machine." Bolsonaro became so unnerved by
Mandetta's briefings and his growing popularity that at one
point he moved the press conferences to the presidential palace
and allowed Mandetta to speak only briefly at the end. "Nobody
should forget that I'm the president," Bolsonaro declared
furiously.

Mandetta resisted calls for his resignation—"a doctor does
not abandon his patient"became his refrain—forcing Bolsonaro
to fire him on April 16. Mandetta's replacement, Nelson Teich,
lasted less than a month, quitting in protest after the president pressured him to state publicly that hydroxychloroquine
was an effective treatment. While Mandetta's approval rating at
the time of his departure stood at 76 percent, some criticized
him for grandstanding and for doing little beyond speaking out
about the disease. But for Mandetta, this was an essential role.
With no medical interventions available, the only way to fight
the disease was with information, to use his credibility and
influence to convince people to observe social distancing and to
wear masks.

Ultimately, Mandetta's efforts to counter Bolsonaro's narrative were only partially successful, which explains why Brazil
had one of the highest rates of COVID infection in the world.
For Mandetta, the threat to democracy in Brazil posed by Bolsonaro's response to COVID-19 was existential. The president's intransigence, his refusal to acknowledge or address the
health risks to the population, his sheer incompetence, and his
hostility toward vaccines prolonged suffering and death. The
damage done to the institutions that sustain Brazilian democracy has also been profound, and may be Bolsonaro's enduring

78   legacy. Bolsonaro is emblematic of a new generation of populist autocrats who embrace and even celebrate a kind of willful
ignorance that borders on nihilism, Mandetta fears. "They don't
care about rules and they don't care about whatever came before
them," Mandetta noted. "The pandemic really showed this. They
practice an ideology we don't know or have a name for. It's just a
new way to not care about anything. Not even lives matter."

In 2018, a full year before the first inklings of the new
disease emerged in Wuhan, the WHO published a guidance
to governments on communicating during a pandemic. The
report recommended a specific style of crisis communication,
which included listening carefully to concerns of impacted
populations. "The latest and most accurate information must
be conveyed frequently, and uncertainties related to an epidemic must be acknowledged in order to maintain credibility
and public trust," the report noted. It called on governments
to combat rumors by combining listening and monitoring and
then responding rapidly whenever false or misleading information began to spread. The WHO was often criticized for its
weak response to the pandemic, but its guidance on communication was spot on.

But instead of leveling with their citizens, explaining the
threat, justifying the government response, and rallying the
population to support the common cause, leaders of three of the
world's leading democracies disrupted the flow of critical information in order to advance government narratives grounded
in lies. Yes lockdowns, mask mandates, and social distancing
requirements are restrictions on negative liberty, and restraints
on the freedom that citizens generally enjoy in a democracy.
But suppressing critical information during a public health

emergency is a threat to democracy itself, because it undermines the informed decisionmaking that is at the heart of positive liberty.

This was certainly Olivia Troye's experience in the White House. In the months she spent helping to spearhead the nation's response to COVID, Troye was unable to counter the narrative that was coming from President Trump, namely that COVID-19 posed a limited threat to public health and would disappear like magic. Troye's contrary views were not actively suppressed, but she was unable to gain a foothold in an information environment defined by chaos in which the president and his top advisors were undermining any sort of rational policymaking process. By the summer, Troye had become so disillusioned with the COVID response, including what she saw as the vice president's pandering, that she decided she had to resign—not just from the White House but from the Department of Homeland Security from where she had been detailed. She later endorsed Joe Biden for president. "The problem did not go away when Trump lost the election," Troye believes. "We are living the legacy today."

State Surveillance

Kirsten Han understands that the government of her native Singapore wants to keep tabs on the population to bring COVID-19 under control. She is willing to do her part to defeat the disease. But nobody ever asked if she minded her every movement being tracked by CCTV the moment she steps outside. There was no consultation before it became necessary to scan a Quick Response (QR) code on her cell phone to enter a store. No official has satisfactorily explained what the government is going to do with all the information it is collecting from a contact tracing app and key fob, known locally as a token, that she is being asked to use. The government just expects residents to comply.

How much freedom from government intrusion in the form of location tracking and sharing of private medical data should an individual tolerate in the name of public health? Who should decide how much data to collect, who can use it, where to store it, and for how long? Should citizens have the right to opt out if they believe governments have overstepped the mark?

In the first months of the pandemic these questions and others relating to privacy were frequently brushed aside as many countries around the world scrambled to monitor the spread of a disease they barely understood. Governments reached for technologies often designed for spying and law enforcement to tackle a health crisis. Privacy advocates feared such "techno-solutionism," the belief that there's a tech fix for everything, would drag the world further down the path to a government and corporate surveillance hell. Geolocation through mobile devices, facial recognition, and temperature scanners in public places; digital vaccination certificates; QR codes on phones as the price of access to services and travel, all became normalized during the pandemic.

When philosopher Isaiah Berlin was contemplating encroachments on a citizen's negative liberty, he was living in a world where pervasive mass surveillance was not scalable; Cold War technology required a state to deploy an army of human spies and informants alongside electronic surveillance equipment to fully track just one individual. The data-sucking tools of the COVID digital age make the fears of loss of individual privacy back then seem quaint.

Ironically, restrictions on physical movement during the pandemic forced people even deeper into the arms of technology. Locked-down workers pumped billions of dollars into the tech sector by conducting business over upstart platforms like Zoom, which quickly became a mainstay of global video-conferencing. People ordered everything from food to frivolities for home delivery through Amazon, which meticulously recorded its customers' online lives and its employees' physical

82   movements in the name of efficiency. Bedrooms were turned
       into schoolrooms, and in order to graduate, students were some-
       times obliged to download intrusive remote exam software such
       as Proctorio or ExamSoft, which monitors a student's face and
       keystrokes. The pandemic produced what is arguably the big-
       gest surrender of individual data in human history. This data
       was harvested and used by autocracies like China, by partially
       free countries like Singapore, and by full democracies such as
       Israel and Norway. In all of them citizens were variously coerced
       or cajoled into giving up personal information. They were told it
       was necessary and temporary. It may turn out to be neither.

           In the case of Singapore, Han, a journalist, blogger, and
       rights activist, has deep concerns. She wants to know why the
       authorities sucked up so much personal information and what
       they are doing with it. She wants to know who has access to it.
       She wants to know how securely it is being stored and for how
       long. She wants to know what recourse people have if they were
       misidentified as infected. The government has not provided
       adequate answers.

           Singapore has the structures and trappings of a Western
       liberal democracy but it has had only three leaders, all from the
       same party, since independence from Britain in 1959. And two
       of those were father and son. The social contract for the island's
       nearly 6 million inhabitants is simple: a large measure of secu-
       rity and prosperity compared with the rest of Southeast Asia
       in return for curtailed political freedoms including little tol-
       erance of sustained opposition or criticism of Prime Minister
       Lee Hsien Loong, son of independence leader Lee Kuan Yew, and
       his People's Action Party. Singapore is wealthy but its economy
       is heavily dependent on global trade, finance, shipping, and

tourism, with 68 million passengers a year flowing through its
Changi airport.

Long before the advent of digital surveillance technology, the city-state had enforced order through public education, a co-opted media, and policing that curbed everything from street crime to spitting, littering, and jaywalking.

Singapore was one of the few countries ready for the pandemic. It had built up contact tracing capabilities to deal with the Severe Acute Respiratory Syndrome (SARS) outbreak in 2003 and the H1N1 swine flu in 2009.

After the first cases of COVID-19 were confirmed in January 2020, the government deployed human contact tracers but quickly realized it needed technology to help speed up the process. By March it had developed a Bluetooth-enabled phone app called TraceTogether. The app works by swapping anonymized identifiers between phones that come near each other. If a user has been diagnosed with COVID-19, that information is uploaded to their phone and those who come into contact with that person are alerted. The app has some important privacy safeguards. User information is stored on the phone itself, not in a central database, and the technology is open source so developers abroad can examine and copy it. Privacy experts say Bluetooth's proximity tracing is less invasive of privacy than location tracing using a smartphone's own GPS chip where the data is sent to a centralized system. Rivals Apple and Google even worked together to develop a similar app, the Exposure Notifications System, which has been adopted in some forty countries.

The app was immediately made mandatory for Singapore's large migrant worker population. The virus had raged through dormitories housing thousands of male laborers who worked

84   in construction and manufacturing. The workers, mainly from the Indian subcontinent and China, were placed in lockdown for months.

But downloading TraceTogether onto a phone was voluntary for the rest of the island's residents. For those who did not have a smartphone, the government offered tokens that resemble key fobs that did the same thing.

Adoption rates were low, however, and that was a problem because to be an effective epidemiological tool, contact tracing apps need at least two-thirds of the population to use them. So the government announced that the TraceTogether would eventually become compulsory as part of an easing of restrictions on movement for anyone wanting to enter a public venue.

"There's not really a culture of protest or resistance against the government. A lot of things are very top-down and normalized in that way. So I think it was already interesting that when they first launched TraceTogether, so few people used it. I think that already, that is a very Singaporean way of showing resistance, just not adopting it. And adoption has shot up now, but that's because they said they were going to make it mandatory. So it wasn't acceptance that led people to download TraceTogether. It was the news that you're going to need it to get around that made people get it," Han said. Any sense that people had preserved their privacy was short lived. Shortly after introducing TraceTogether, the government unveiled SafeEntry, a QR code needed to enter public spaces, shops, and offices. "TraceTogether doesn't track your location, but SafeEntry does. And as long as you're combining these two systems, it's not really honest to keep saying that TraceTogether doesn't track your location, because while that's technically not lying, practically, they can track your location through SafeEntry," Han added.

The QR entry codes sprouted everywhere from April 2020. Han explained: "If I track my day and I go to a shopping mall, I will scan to go into the shopping mall. Then once I'm in the mall, if I wanted to go and have lunch, I'll scan before I go into the restaurant, inside the mall. And then, if after lunch, I want to go to the supermarket to buy something, I would scan to go inside the supermarket. And so you would scan to go into pretty much every single shop in the mall."

Some people might have considered this a small price to pay for the ability to even go into a mall in the middle of 2020 when much of Europe and the Americas were under lockdown. But again, where does all that data go and who uses it?

"It goes to a government server," Han said. "And that's about as far as we know. I think every twenty-one days or so the data might get purged because presumably after that amount of time, it's no longer useful for contract tracing anyway. But there's no independent oversight mechanism that would check that they've really done that. So it's taking the government's word for it that they're handling it properly."

That trust proved to be misguided. In January 2021, the government acknowledged that the police had always had the power to obtain such information in criminal investigations and had already done so in one murder probe. It did not say how the police had retrieved the information from the ministry of health, who had decrypted it, and who oversaw and authorized the whole process, or what recourse there would be for those whose information had been wrongfully grabbed.

86   The revelations dealt another blow to public trust and added to the unease felt by many privacy advocates in the fifty or more countries that had also introduced digital trackers. TraceTogether was already on a slippery privacy slope. When first introduced, users were required to give a phone number; then, later, without great fanfare, they were told they needed to give their national identification card number to register.

Could the government be trusted to keep their data safe? Hackers had already stolen health records, first in 2018 and again in the following year.

"We had this massive hack where 1.5 million people's medical data was accessed," Han said. "And then we've had other cases, one case where the entire HIV registry with names and addresses of people with HIV in Singapore was leaked."

Like many Singaporeans, Han expresses her opposition carefully and indirectly. "So on the one hand we had these security concerns," she notes. "On the other hand, we have privacy concerns. And I think in Singapore, we just haven't had enough chance to talk about it in a way that would make a difference. Often we are talking about it because it's already been implemented, but we don't get to talk about it before."

A police drone whirs up to the sixteenth floor of a Tel Aviv apartment building and hovers outside a window. A woman in a pink top and headscarf appears holding a cell phone in her left hand. With her right she waves nervously at the camera. She has been summoned to the window by a police phone call. They want to see that she is at home and observing quarantine. The police have made the footage available to the national media. They

are keen to show off their new technology. It's mid-April 2020,
and Israel is in the grip of a first wave of COVID-19. Police have
already knocked on one hundred thousand doors checking on
known cases and on Israelis who have returned home from hot
spots like Europe. It has strained their resources. The country
is a high-tech hub once dubbed "Silicon Wadi," so naturally it
would turn to technology to help enforce lockdown, quarantine,
social distancing, and mask-wearing regulations to keep pressure off its cash-strapped public health system and hospitals.

It was surveillance in the service of health. Who could
object to a spy-in-the-sky under those very public conditions?
What many citizens did not initially know, however, was that
the country's domestic intelligence agency was already tracking
them covertly. Israel, which styles itself as the Middle East's
only true democracy, had decided to tackle a public health emergency as a security threat.

At the end of February 2020, the coronavirus hit a country
in political turmoil. Prime Minister Benjamin Netanyahu was
clinging to power while fending off corruption charges. Voters
had gone to the polls three times in a year but general elections
had failed to deliver a clear result that would allow anything
other than a caretaker government and weak parliament.

Compared with the security services, the health care system
had been underfunded for years. There was no modern legal
provision for pandemic control or privacy protection in Israel.
In times of crisis, the Jewish state has always turned to its security forces. It did not need to declare a general state of emergency. The country has been under one since independence in
1948. All the authorities needed to do was dust off Section 20 of

88   the Public Health Ordinance introduced under British Mandate
rule to issue sweeping anti-pandemic measures such as quarantining and contact tracing.

Human contact tracers were deployed but the government
needed more information faster. Netanyahu turned to the General Security Service, better known by its Hebrew acronym
Shabak or Shin Bet, which reports directly to his office. The
Shin Bet did not need to hack Israelis' phones or force them to
download some COVID-19 app. It was already sitting on a trove
of mobile phone location data gathered as part of counterterrorism operations. It knew where Israelis, and Palestinians for
that matter, had been and who they had met.

Nicknamed "The Tool," the technology scooped up metadata from anyone using telecommunications in Israel and the
occupied Palestinian territories. "The GSS operates a huge
secret intelligence database, which collects information about
all citizens of the State of Israel. All conversations, all text
messages, all locations, all the time," the daily *Yediot Ahronot*
revealed in March 2020.

The government rushed to defend its use of The Tool,
calling it a lifesaver, and sought to reassure Israelis, who traditionally place great faith in the armed forces and intelligence
services, that their data was not being exploited.

But privacy advocates challenged Netanyahu's emergency
regulations all the way to the Supreme Court and won a partial
victory. The government was ordered to place limits on health
information gathered by the technology and delete information
after a certain time. Critics contended that there was still insuf-
ficient oversight of how Shin Bet handled the information or
whether it deleted it.

In tandem with The Tool, the Health Ministry released a contact tracing app on March 22 called HaMagen (the Shield), which relied on user consent. The app collected location data and cross-referenced it with that of confirmed COVID-19 cases. But data input and tracking errors in the open code app discouraged many Israelis from downloading it, lessening its effectiveness as a tracing tool. Also, the app could only be used on smartphones, which effectively ruled out its deployment among the million ultra-Orthodox Jews, about 12 percent of the Israeli population, who for largely religious reasons avoid the internet and use older-style mobile phones. In defiance of health regulations, the community also held large gatherings such as weddings and funerals, making it prone to higher spread rates.

The government repeatedly defended its use of The Tool in court, and when a second wave of coronavirus swept Israel in mid-2020, it again brought in Shin Bet. Despite more legal challenges from civil society, the law continued into 2021.

"The digital contact tracing conducted by the Shabak is here to stay," according to Tehilla Shwartz Altshuler, a senior fellow at the Israel Democracy Institute, a think tank in Jerusalem. "The government has no intention to stop using it, even though the more we go on with the pandemic, the less efficient this kind of particular technology is."

Many Israelis became frustrated with their government's handling of the crisis and complained that the tracking tools were inaccurate. A mistake meant someone could be ordered into two weeks of isolation unjustifiably. Geolocation inside residential buildings is problematic, too, and can place an infected person in the wrong apartment. Shwartz Altshuler estimates that more

90   than one hundred thousand people were mistakenly ordered to self-isolate because of errors with the technology.

In October 2020, the State Comptroller's Office issued a damning interim report showing that only 3.5 percent of people identified by Shin Bet as having come in contact with COVID patients were found to have the virus. It said it would have been better to use human rather than digital tracking.

A surveillance state is effective, however, at amassing mountains of data, the lifeblood of medical and artificial intelligence researchers. As a third wave of the virus washed over Israel in late 2020, Prime Minister Netanyahu, facing a fourth general election in two years in March 2021, pulled out all the stops to procure vaccines. He struck a deal for delivery of the Pfizer-BioNTech vaccine by promising to share with Pfizer clinical data on its impact. The bargain was quickly dubbed "data for doses" by the press and criticized by privacy experts who warned about the risks of the secondary use of such huge health datasets. The data is anonymized but little is known about how it will be used and what guarantees will be made that it won't be de-anonymized (which is technically possible). The government released a redacted copy of the agreement with Pfizer, which left many questions for privacy advocates about data storage and use unanswered. Israel has a centralized and digitized health care system and the government has the vaccination history of every citizen.

"This is what they've promised Pfizer, an access to this kind of dataset without my consent," Shwartz Altshuler added.

The nexus between Israel's state security apparatus and the commercial security industry is tight. The country is home to

some of the most prominent and controversial spyware and
hacking software makers on the planet.

As intelligence officers monitored citizens at home in the
early days of the outbreak, Israeli business executives turned
abroad to pitch their wares. They sensed an opportunity to
move in on a global spyware business estimated to be worth $3.6
billion by research firm MarketsandMarkets by adapting their
technologies for the burgeoning contact tracing market.

NSO Group, known for developing and selling governments
access to its Pegasus spyware, pushed a system called Fleming.
"Fleming features an advanced mapping tool that identifies
the spread of coronavirus in real-time, empowering health and
other government officials to make informed decisions, backed
by data, to quickly mitigate the pandemic," the company said
on its website. "The technology anonymizes all data inputted
by the operator, which adds an additional layer of privacy and
security," it added. One pitch was to Saudi Arabia, which is suspected of using Pegasus to tap communications of journalists
and dissidents including murdered *Washington Post* columnist
Jamal Khashoggi. NSO denies its products were so used.

It is not clear how many states have adopted the new NSO
technology but the company itself says: "Fleming is already being
operated by countries around the world as health officials work to
stop the spread of COVID-19 and keep citizens safe and healthy."

Another Israeli company, Cellebrite, also got in on the
act. Its Universal Forensic Extraction Device is already used
by law enforcement around the world to crack mobile phones.
By plugging the software into the phone of someone infected
with COVID-19, authorities could download the patient's locations and contacts. This would make it easier for authorities to

92   "quarantine the right people," the company wrote in an April 22,
2020, email pitch to the police in New Delhi, India, which was
seen by Reuters. "We do not need the phone passcode to collect
the data," the salesperson boasted. Delhi police said they did not
take up the offer.

At least eight surveillance and cyber-intelligence firms
have tried to sell their repurposed wares to track the pandemic,
Reuters reported, but the companies would not disclose which
countries had bought their products.

Many nations were already armed with an array of surveillance tools before COVID-19, but as the virus spread, governments wanted to show anxious populations they were in
control. More than fifty countries deployed smartphone apps
for contact tracing or quarantine monitoring within the first
few months of the outbreak.

The way a society responded largely depended on its preex-
isting digital culture. That ranged from China, which saw data
gathering as a mass utility rather than something that needed
to be restricted, to the European Union, which has enacted laws,
among them the General Data Protection Regulation (GDPR),
to help shield citizens from intrusive state and corporate
technologies.

China rolled out tracking and quarantine compliance technologies within weeks of the outbreak, co-opting its commercial tech giants and adding their data haul to its already
overflowing information treasure chest, which includes a burgeoning DNA databank. China Mobile pushed out a tracking
service, and Baidu developed an AI program to spot individuals
ignoring the mask mandate. The facial recognition firm Megvii
introduced a temperature scanner.

An app called "Close Contact Detector" allowed users of the ubiquitous payment service Alipay and the social media platform WeChat to scan a QR code to monitor contact with infected people. Some apps gave users green, yellow, and red health codes, which, if inspected by an official, could determine whether the phone owner was allowed to enter public spaces or to be sent off to quarantine. All of these technologies and the private biomedical data that they sucked up were presented as virtuous, and necessary to combat the spread of infection.

"In the era of big data and the internet, the movements of each person can be clearly seen. So we are different from the SARS time now," Li Lanjuan, an advisor to the National Health Commission, said in an interview with Chinese state TV. "With such new technologies, we should make full use of them to find and contain the source of infection."

Privacy and data security were not even an afterthought. Citizens were required to register national ID and phone numbers and this data was merged with information culled from telecommunications firms, transport agencies, health care providers, and state-owned enterprises. Some health records leaked onto the internet and the *New York Times* reported that the Alipay Health Code app shared information with the police.

Democracies like South Korea and Taiwan deployed a biomedical data dragnet with more safeguards than China, but with levels of intrusion that would likely be unacceptable in many Western countries and Japan. Widespread and rapid testing helped South Korea and Taiwan keep the pandemic under control, but this was rolled out alongside a tracking regime that exposed individuals' most personal details. South Korea had mechanisms in place from tackling a Middle East Respiratory

94   Syndrome (MERS) outbreak in 2015. Health officials had the power to collect information without a warrant on confirmed and suspected cases. They pulled surveillance camera footage, phone location data, and credit card records and combined it with information from in-person interviews. The government published some of this data, anonymized, on websites and via text messages to alert the public.

"Patient No.12 had booked Seats E13 and E14 for a 5:30 p.m. showing of the South Korean film, *The Man Standing Next*," read one post. "Before grabbing a 12:40 p.m. train, patient No.17 dined at a soft-tofu restaurant in Seoul," read another.

Officials defended such disclosures as necessary and argued that without them the disease would have spread even more rapidly. They also noted that there was a limit on how long authorities could store the data, which would have to be deleted after it had been used.

Most states could not go down the route of blanket surveillance and hermetic confinement as China did, but many took significant steps in that direction. Saudi Arabia, Bahrain, and Qatar made apps for those in quarantine mandatory. India, the world's biggest democracy, rushed out several apps without clear legislative protections for privacy. The most widely used Bluetooth app, Aarogya Setu, was not made compulsory for everybody, although employers and workers were ordered to use it and life without the app became difficult.

"When I go to the bank, before I enter, I need to show that I have it on my phone. Even when I visit stores I have to show it," said Amber Sinha, executive director of the Centre for Internet and Society (CIS) in India. "Even though it has not been made mandatory for a number of things the market demands it."

The southern Indian state of Karnataka required those in self-isolation to send a selfie, initially every hour, with geolocation metadata through its Quarantine Watch app to prove they were at home. Poland and Russia had similar regulations requiring those in self-isolation to upload selfies. Australia, which had relied on stringent lockdowns and mandatory hotel quarantine to withstand the initial waves of COVID, grabbed for intrusive technology as the Delta variant ran through its largely unvaccinated population. In August 2021, travelers to the state of South Australia quarantining at home had to download an app that uses geolocation and facial recognition to ensure they stay there. The app contacts users at random who then have fifteen minutes to prove they are where they are supposed to be. Under the headline "Australia Traded Away Too Much Liberty," *Atlantic* writer Conor Friedersdorf called the state's app "as Orwellian as any in the free world to enforce its quarantine rules."

The rush to produce technological solutions for tracking and tracing and health regulation enforcement unnerved privacy defenders and prompted some developers to search for the least privacy-harming solutions.

"Apps are notorious for their lack of security and privacy at the best of times," said Lucy Purdon, policy director of the London-based advocacy organization Privacy International. She said public trust and confidence that personal data would not be misused were vital for tech solutions to work and many countries had failed that test. "A real mess has been made of the whole contact tracing thing through an app, in quite a lot of countries," she added.

In an effort to allay privacy fears, a team of Swiss engineers led an international consortium to produce an opt-in Bluetooth tracing app called DP-3T, or Decentralized Privacy-Preserving Proximity Tracing. It did not send information to the government and let users choose whether to share their phone number. If they opted to do so, their phone would automatically exchange information with nearby phones using the same system and alert users who had been in close proximity with anyone who was infected. By late April 2020, Apple and Google developed a notification system for their respective iOS and Android devices, which maximized security and privacy and which did not upload user information automatically to a company or government central server. Many Western governments rolled out apps built on the Application Programming Interface (API) of one of these two systems. They included Germany and Japan, whose post–World War II histories have contributed to a culture that is suspicious of government intrusion and extremely protective of personal privacy. The technology in both systems offered better privacy protections than GPS-based centralized storage systems, but it can still be hacked by a determined attacker.

          Looking for such vulnerabilities in apps is part of Claudio Guarnieri's job. As head of Amnesty International's Security Lab, he focused first on those countries that were rushing out mandatory apps. That's when Qatar caught his eye. In May 2020, the Persian Gulf emirate rolled out its Ehteraz app that required access to files on the phone and permanent use of its GPS and Bluetooth capabilities to carry out tracking. Failure to install the app was punishable with a fine of up to $55,000 or three years in prison.

Guarnieri unearthed a flaw in the app's QR code that would have allowed hackers to access a user's complete health data and location. He contacted the Qatari government with the news. "Thankfully we managed to intervene quickly, and the authorities, to their credit, responded quickly too," he said. They patched the flaw.

Guarnieri was also hot on the trail of an app that Norway had launched in April 2020. Prime Minister Erna Solberg urged Norwegians to download the Smittestopp (stop infection) app so that "we can open up society more and get our freedom back." Within two weeks, one-fifth of the adult population had done just that. The app continuously sent location data to a government database for analysis. The Norwegian Institute of Public Health loved it. It helped them understand how lockdowns and social distancing measures were working. Technologists like Guarnieri weren't so happy. In May, three hundred Norwegian security, privacy, and tech experts decided to go public and issued a statement on the open platform Medium warning of the "unprecedented surveillance" of society.

In June, the Norwegian Data Protection Authority issued a temporary ban on the app and the Institute of Public Health stopped collecting data from some 600,000 active users and deleted all data on its Azure cloud server. The Institute's deputy director general was furious. "It's good for democracy to have a huge debate when we collect this amount of data," said Gun Peggy Knudsen. "But I am surprised that the critics, primarily tech people in Norway, are focusing so much on the privacy side and not on how can we handle public health during the coronavirus outbreak."

98   The Data Protection Authority's response was that the health authorities had not proved the tool's effectiveness and had denied citizens the ability to control how their data was used. "The app was introduced in what you might call a warlike situation," said Simen Sommerfeldt, one of the tech experts who organized the public statement. He told the *New York Times* that the disease was more like a long-term "new normal." In which case, "we can't have an app that is so invasive of privacy. . . . We need to protect human rights even in this situation," he added.

The campaign worked. At the end of 2020, the government reintroduced a completely overhauled app based on the Apple-Google API, with no centralized tracking and which was completely voluntary.

The rare victory in Norway obscured the massive erosion of privacy around the world. Digital authoritarianism—the use of technology to control and shape the behavior of citizens—expanded almost everywhere in the name of protecting public health.

Contact apps are just a small part of a bigger problem, according to Ron Deibert, director of the Citizen Lab at the University of Toronto's Munk School, which monitors surveillance technology. He sees the whole unregulated, data-leaking infrastructure of the internet as a threat to civil liberties. "When it comes to digital technologies and COVID-19, by far the vast majority of discussion has focused on contact-tracing applications," Deibert explained. "Although important, this narrow focus has obscured more fundamental and far-reaching effects at the intersection of digital technology, surveillance, and pandemic response. "Largely without public debate—and absent

any new safeguards—we've become even more dependent on a
technological ecosystem that is notoriously insecure."

The COVID-19 pandemic could do for biomedical surveillance what 9/11 did for wiretapping. The response to the attacks
on the Twin Towers and Pentagon was to declare war on a threat,
terrorism, and use whatever tools were at hand to combat the
enemy. If the tools did not exist, the government built them.
One lasting legislative outcome was the USA Patriot Act, which
endowed state agencies with unprecedented legal and technological powers of surveillance. Many of the curtailments of personal freedom of movement and privacy that were promised as
temporary have become permanent. The days when passengers
could board a flight without having to give up personal details
and travel plans to a commercial airline and the government are
a distant memory. Intrusion into the private lives of citizens has
been normalized. Information about where a person goes, who
they go with, and how long they stay is now a precondition for
buying a plane ticket. As the "War on Terror" advanced, whis-
tleblowers revealed how all communications, not just those of
suspects, could be tapped and individuals' data mined, by the
NSA or security agencies around the world.

Citizens' digital exhaust from everyday interactions in the
online world of social connection, commerce, leisure, travel,
and education has billowed in the intervening two decades. In
2018, it was revealed how a commercial enterprise, Cambridge
Analytica, could buy users' data from Facebook without their
knowledge and monetize it. Such data is available to authorities
and can be combined with intrusive spying measures to quickly
and cheaply compile a personal dossier not for a handful of targets as in the days of J. Edgar Hoover's FBI or East Germany's

100   Stasi, but for millions. These are heady days for the surveillance
       state and its commercial partners.

       Political institutions, laws, societal norms, and bioethics
       have not kept pace with the technology. Citizens learn all too
       often after the fact what governments and corporations have
       been doing with their data.

       Viewed through the lens of negative liberty, the long-term
       implications of this intrusion into private lives are worrying.
       Some democratic governments have tried, if only weakly, to
       make a case for deploying mass surveillance to deal with health
       emergencies, disease outbreaks, and natural disasters to save
       lives. But the question remains: what prevents authorities from
       deploying the same technologies to spy on political opponents,
       dissidents, and anti-government protesters? Without the
       state's vigorous guaranteeing of citizens' positive rights to con-
       trol and oversee the collection and use of their data, the answer
       is precious little.

       "It has completely normalized mobile phone use in contact
       tracing for disease surveillance and I do think that does set a
       dangerous precedent," said Amber Sinha of India's CIS. "When-
       ever we have even a small outbreak, a flu outbreak of any kind
       I do feel that the first response is going to be to use Bluetooth
       apps."

       The one thing COVID-19 has done is show the glaring need
       for updated privacy laws and new regulatory and ethics frame-
       works to protect citizens' data, whether from governments or
       from corporations feeding their revenue-generating algorithms
       off users' most personal information. Users are asked to trust
       that both governments and companies have their interests at

heart without ever being allowed to peer into their technology
black box.

"You can't trust technology to solve all your problems. I think this is a huge lesson, because some of those technologies are very, very, harmful to privacy," said the Israel Democracy Institute's Shwartz Altshuler.

More than 130 countries have some form of constitutional safeguards or regulations on privacy or data protection but hardly any respected or implemented them. "It is striking how normalized monitoring a person's movement and health have become acceptable practices, irrespective of a country's political system," said Binoy Kampmark, a lecturer at Melbourne's RMIT university, who tracks privacy. "Pandemic biopower, in other words, is here to stay, given the prospect of future pandemics and COVID strains. The coronavirus pandemic has indelibly transformed the relationship between living bodies, citizenry, and the entities that govern us."

Trust Me

In the first few months of the pandemic, governments around the world censored critical information, while seeking to discredit, marginalize, or undermine those who challenged their authority. The infodemic—the flood of misinformation, lies, rumors, and half-truths that created confusion and undermined the global response—was the result. The infodemic also fed the collapse in trust, which is a government's most important asset during a public health emergency. This is because the least liberty-restricting approach to protecting public health in a pandemic is to persuade people to change their behavior based on science. Without trust—trust in the media, trust in experts, and trust in political leaders—the use of persuasion becomes impossible. What is left is coercion or denialism.

Local journalism—journalists who know their communities and live among the people they cover—is the most trusted source of information for many people around the world. The pandemic-related decline of local news organizations is the focus of the next chapter. But the collapse of trust was also

fueled by a media environment in which information about
public health was distorted and weaponized as part of deliberate political strategies. This was especially true in the United
States, where Charles Loftus, a retired cop and current crimi-
nology professor at Arizona State University, sought to make
critical health decisions after contracting COVID. Loftus is a
highly engaged citizen and discriminating consumer of information. Yet he found himself sucked down a rabbit hole of misinformation that led him to embrace conspiracy theories linked
to his support for President Trump.

Loftus, who goes by Charlie and exudes an unfussy friendli-
ness, prides himself on the variety of news sources he consumes.
"Like I tell my students, there's media and every single one has
a bias," Loftus asserts. "You need to watch a variety of news, the
right, the left, the middle, the Christian, the Jewish, even RT
News. They hate America. But they report stuff that you'll never
see in American news." (RT is a Russian-government funded
propaganda network.)

But if one single news organization captures Loftus's world-
view, it's Fox News. In fact, Fox has been Loftus's go-to source
since the 9/11 terrorist attacks in New York City and Washington. Soon after the planes hit, Loftus flipped from CNN to
Fox. He found the coverage more straightforward, and particularly appreciated anchors like Shepard Smith, who reminded
him of Walter Cronkite with his just-the-facts style. Loftus
liked the greater reliance on law enforcement and military commentators, with whom he identified. Most days he watches Fox
Business and listens to Fox Headline News in his car.

While Loftus describes himself as a conservative and
Trump supporter, he says his political outlook is shaped in part

by his career in law enforcement. "I think cops have a little bit different view on the world than most people because of what they see and what they have to do," Loftus explained. After graduating from the police academy at nineteen and working briefly at a jail, Loftus got a job with the ASU University Police. One of the perks of his job was a tuition waiver, which Loftus parlayed into a college degree and a PhD. He also met his wife, Rebecca, at ASU. She was a student worker at the campus police department, where she served as a dispatcher. She went on to become a probation officer specializing in sex offenders.

In 2008, after retiring from the campus police force, Loftus took a position at the Arizona attorney general's office where he investigated organized crime, drug trafficking, and public corruption, including a case against Western Union for alleged money laundering to Mexico that resulted in a $94-million settlement in 2010. In 2016, Loftus joined Arizona's Department of Economic Security, which functions as a statewide social services agency, but also has a small law enforcement division that investigates economic crimes and provides security for the Department's nearly 8,000 employees. He was forced out after only eight months and was later investigated by the Arizona Department of Public Safety for irregularities in the purchase of the ammunition and firearms, including fifty handguns and 80,000 rounds that were stored under a desk in a basement. Loftus said he purchased the guns and ammo legally, in order to ensure agents had adequate supplies, and a state audit later cleared him of wrongdoing. After a brief and unsuccessful run for the Arizona State Senate in 2018, Loftus turned to teaching full-time.

Loftus's father, who went by Eddie and was the son of a Texas cowboy and a Mexican immigrant, was a lifelong Democrat, and

Charlie was a registered Democrat for more than thirty years. In 2008, Loftus voted for John McCain because he was a war hero and Arizona icon though he admired Barack Obama as a gifted orator. Later, though, Loftus came to disdain Obama who he believes is a closet socialist who misled the American public about his true ideology. Loftus's list of grievances reflects those often trumpeted by conservative media, among them that Obama cavorted with radicals and he failed to release his college transcripts. (Loftus suspects he didn't want the world to know that he studied Marxism.) Loftus eventually concluded that Obama "fundamentally wanted to change America." By the end of Obama's presidency, Loftus had switched his party affiliation from Democrat to Republican.

In this context he saw Trump as a breath of fresh air. Mostly Loftus liked his tough talk, including Trump's policies on immigration. Given his own background, Loftus certainly did not believe that all Mexicans were rapists. But he does believe that the immigration "industry" is out of control and that illegal immigration is taking a terrible toll on Arizona's economy. He has also seen up close the violence that the transborder drug trade has wrought.

Loftus believes that Trump had some significant achievements as president, including putting conservative judges on the Supreme Court and in the Ninth Circuit and strengthening US support for the right-wing government in Israel, a country where Loftus leads a study abroad program each year focused on counterterrorism. In fact, it was because of these security relationships that Loftus learned early on about the new virus spreading in Wuhan, China. A brief item in a private intelligence report to which he subscribes piqued his interest. Then,

106 in mid-January 2020, "a member of the ASU community" who
had recently returned from Wuhan became one of the first diagnosed cases in the US.

Loftus's political support for Trump caused him to give the
president the benefit of the doubt in terms of his response to
the pandemic. He believes that Trump initially got bad advice
from experts, who downplayed the risk of the disease. (Based
on the account of Olivia Troye and many others, we know that
Trump resisted any expert guidance and in fact contributed
immensely to the information chaos that engulfed the White
House during the initial phase.) Loftus accepts that at some
point Trump began to actively downplay the risk in order to try
and keep the economy open.

Loftus also had mixed feelings about his personal risk of
contracting COVID. When the virus first emerged, he stopped
taking one of his regular medications because he was concerned that it might weaken his immunity. While he does not
believe masks are particularly effective, he did eventually decide
to wear one. Despite these efforts, Loftus contracted COVID
in November 2020. He thinks he was infected during a routine
medical procedure at a local hospital. His decisions about how
to treat the disease were deeply informed by his views that any
information coming from government agencies and the media
is inherently unreliable.

After being told by his doctor to monitor his symptoms
and finding no useful treatments on the CDC website, Loftus
decided, based in part on the president's affirmations, to take
an antimalarial medicine. The medication he took was called
atovaquone/proguanil, which he believed to be similar to
hydroxychloroquine. He happened to have the drug on hand

because of a recent trip to Ethiopia, where he had advised the government on counterterror measures. Loftus found his symptoms dissipated and believes the drug cured him. He was well aware that the Food and Drug Administration advised against taking hydroxychloroquine; that it had little medical value and created some risk. He dismissed the guidance out of hand.

Reflecting on his own career as a cop as "the guy tapping people's phones and putting listening devices in their cars and TVs," Loftus explained why he had so little confidence in government pronouncements. "I come from government. And I don't trust the government."

On February 15, 2020, before an audience of foreign policy experts at the Munich Security Conference in Germany, WHO Director General Tedros Adhanom Ghebreyesus declared, "We're not just fighting an epidemic. We are fighting an infodemic." Referring to the rumors, lies, and conspiracy theories, circulating online and through the media, Tedros lamented that these spread "faster and more easily than this virus."

Two months later, on April 14, at a time when there were 2 million cases of COVID-19 around the world and 120,000 people had already died, UN Secretary-General António Guterres announced the creation of a special communications project to fight the scourge of misinformation. "Around the world, people are scared," Guterres declared in a video posted to social media channels. "Harmful health advice and snake-oil solutions are proliferating. Falsehoods are filling the airwaves. Wild conspiracy theories are infecting the internet. Hatred is going viral, stigmatizing and vilifying people and groups."

The solution, Guterres asserted, was to flood the internet with "facts and science" that would build trust—trust in science and trust in institutions. "With common cause for common sense and facts, we can defeat COVID-19—and build a healthier, more equitable, just, and resilient world," Guterres concluded.

The international community, Guterres affirmed, needed to find a way to break through. Until effective treatments were developed and a vaccine rolled out, information was just about the only weapon governments had to fight the disease. Accurate, reliable, and timely information could help change personal behavior, and convince people that they needed to abide by lockdowns, maintain social distance, wash their hands, and wear masks. But Guterres's confidence that governments would get behind such an effort was severely misplaced. In fact, from the outset, as we have seen in earlier chapters, far from fighting the infodemic, governments around the world were fueling it. They did this in two ways. First, they used propaganda networks and social media to pump out misinformation that advanced their own position or weakened an adversary's. China's unfounded claim that COVID-19 originated in frozen food imported into the country is one example. Governments consistently censored data about the number of COVID cases to support their contention that the threat was exaggerated. They also made wild claims about miracle cures, including hydroxychloroquine, as a way of suggesting the pandemic would soon end and therefore tough decisions on mitigation measures were unnecessary.

The additional challenge, as the experience of Charles Loftus showed, is that people make decisions based not just on the information they consume, but on the context and

meaning they give to it. Group identity may be more important
than an objective analysis of the facts, and this is particularly
true during periods of conflict and polarization. In the United
States, Trump supporters who got their information directly
from the president's social media or filtered through Fox News
tended to believe the president not because they were irrational
or unsophisticated but because their political identity shaped
their perceptions of reality.

This is why during the first COVID year Americans lived
in several different information ecosystems, which shaped
their perceptions of events, according to a study by the Pew
Research Center. Democrats and Republicans both relied on
partisan media outlets. And a significant portion of the public
got its news directly from President Trump. Democrats turned
to CNN, NPR, MSNBC, the *New York Times*, and the *Washington
Post*. Republicans relied on Fox News (36 percent) and talk radio
(17 percent). While Republicans as a group were much more
likely to be skeptical about the seriousness of the COVID threat,
the numbers rose dramatically among the 30 percent of Republicans who got their news directly from Trump. This group was
"more likely than other Republicans to think the COVID-19
pandemic had been overblown, more likely to see voter fraud
as a significant threat to election integrity and more likely to
render a harsh verdict on the media." The Pew report also noted,
"Republicans turning to Trump for election news expressed
more concern about voter fraud connected to mail-in ballots."

Other studies looked at Fox viewers specifically and examined how the news they consumed on the network shaped their
behavior. Several studies that examined the initial coverage
of the COVID-19 outbreak found that Fox News, along with

110   conservative media as a whole, amplified misinformation and
       sowed confusion about the seriousness of the outbreak and the
       steps that needed to be taken to reduce risk. "We are receiving an
       incredible number of studies and solid data showing that con-
       suming far-right media and social media content was strongly
       associated with low concern about the virus at the onset of the
       pandemic," Irene Pasquetto, the chief editor of the Harvard Ken-
       nedy School Misinformation Review, told the *Washington Post*
       in June. One study concluded that "conservative media use
       (e.g., Fox News) correlated with conspiracy theories including
       believing that some in the CDC were exaggerating the serious-
       ness of the virus to undermine the presidency of Donald Trump."

       A working paper published in May by the National Bureau
       of Economic Research, and which was republished by the Uni-
       versity of Chicago in July, found that Fox viewers were consid-
       erably less likely to follow social distancing guidelines, based
       on an analysis of cell phone data. Another study also published
       by the University of Chicago noted differences in behavior
       between viewers of Sean Hannity, who downplayed the threat
       of the virus in the early days, and Tucker Carlson, who began
       cautioning viewers in early February. The study found that
       viewers of Hannity delayed changing their behavior in relation
       to Carlson viewers. (The study was not subjected to peer review
       and the findings were disputed by Fox.) But a poll commis-
       sioned by The Knight Foundation and Gallup determined that
       nearly 60 percent of the viewers of conservative news outlets
       believed the coronavirus to only be as dangerous or less dan-
       gerous than the flu.

       When Fox was created in 1996, it was modeled after a tra-
       ditional newsroom, with a clear delineation between news and

JOEL SIMON AND ROBERT MAHONEY

opinion. (The Decision Desk, which does polling and election
projection, is a separate division.) While many Fox journalists
had a conservative outlook, they operated within the framework of the journalistic profession and were generally well
regarded by their peers in the mainstream media. Fox journalists reported the news, but they were also there to provide cover
for the morning and evening opinion shows, like *Fox & Friends*,
The O'Reilly Factor, and later *Hannity*, which generated the mass
audiences and the advertising dollars. The Fox business model
relied on the news division to give the entire undertaking credibility and allow the network to respond to criticism about
their standards and accuracy. According to the account of Brian
Stelter in his book *Hoax*, however, the formula broke down with
the Trump presidency, as high-profile journalists like Shepard
Smith left the network while star commentators who had until
then been loosely supervised by network management ran wild.
The news division—the journalism—withered as the commen-
tariat gained the upper hand.

This shifting dynamic created tremendous cognitive dissonance for Fox viewers. They could watch *Fox News Sunday*
host Chris Wallace grill Trump during a July 19 interview for
describing the COVID-19 crisis as "burning embers" at a time
when infections were spiking across the country. (Trump
attributed the increase to the fact that the US had the "best
testing in the world," noting that "if we tested half as much
those numbers would be down.") Or they could tune in to the
opinion shows from Laura Ingraham, Jeanine Pirro, and Sean
Hannity, where the hosts parroted Trump's talking points and
"experts" hawked conspiracy theories, claiming (for example)
that the virus was a bioweapon developed jointly by China and

112   North Korea. There was simply no way for viewers to reconcile
these competing versions of reality, and Trump himself invited
his supporters to pick a side. While he continued to praise the
commentators like Hannity and Ingraham (who called hydroxychloroquine a "game changer"), he lashed out at the journalists
like Wallace and Neil Cavuto, who challenged the drug's efficacy. "Neil Cavuto is an idiot," Trump retweeted after one seg-
ment, adding, "Fox News is no longer the same." By the summer,
some Fox viewers had begun migrating to news outlets like OAN
and Newsmax, which reinforced the president's message that
COVID was waning and wearing a mask was a form of political
surrender without even bothering to have actual journalists to
provide credible cover.

For employees of Fox itself, the dissonance between the wild
claims of the opinion hosts and the experience they were actually living was even more profound. By early March, Fox News
leadership was taking steps to limit COVID infection among
the network's employees, installing sanitizing stations, encouraging handwashing, and increasing the distance between work-
stations in their Manhattan headquarters. By the end of the
month, after several newsroom employees became infected and
New York City moved to lockdown, the station went remote, with
the very same commentators downplaying the risk of infection
now broadcasting from home studios. (Hannity has been broadcasting from his home on Long Island for years.)

As the political context changed, so did the message. By
April 2020, when it was no longer possible to deny the severity
of the outbreak, Fox opinion hosts reinforced Trump's messages
that the virus would fade over the summer; that hydroxychloroquine was a miracle treatment; that the vaccine was coming

soon; that the federal response had been effective; that states
should reopen as soon as possible; that mask-wearing should
be voluntary. The talking points shifted again in May, following
the killing of George Floyd by police in Minneapolis. As protests
exploded across the country, moving the national focus away
from the pandemic and toward a reckoning with racial injus-
tice and police brutality, Fox commentators framed the protests
as evidence of liberal duplicity, arguing that liberals wanted
everyone to stay home, to social distance, and to wear masks,
except when they took to the streets to advance their own political and social agenda. They expanded this critique as the elections approached, until it became a matter of faith among
conservatives that liberals and Democrats were exploiting the
pandemic to attack Trump and disparage his accomplishments,
and looking to shift voting practices in ways that advantaged
the campaign of Joe Biden.

Joan Donovan, an expert on disinformation and the research
director of the Shorenstein Center on Media, Politics, and
Public Policy at Harvard University, has noted, "One thing we
know about the conspiracist mindset is if you are interested in
one conspiracy you tend to be interested in a bunch." Conspiracies can emerge organically—rumors and misinformation can
gain currency and spread—or they can be deliberately manu-
factured by political interests or even governments. Precisely
because the acceptance of one conspiracy—9/11 was an inside
job or the government is covering up UFO sightings—softens
people up to believe the next one, an emerging political strategy
is to throw out a range and see which one sticks.

Loftus prides himself on his sophisticated consumption of
media, and his willingness to reach independent conclusions,

but the way in which he processed and understood information was also deeply informed by the communities of which he
was a part as a former cop and a Trump supporter. His decision,
therefore, to treat his COVID infections with an antimalarial
drug deepened his connection to political forces in Arizona that
were rallying around Trump. Loftus did not believe that COVID
was a hoax, or that those who chose to wear masks had surrendered their autonomy. Yet he sympathized with those who held
these views because, like them, he felt alienated from the political process and believed that Trump was fighting against powerful elites both inside and outside the government who cared
nothing for his freedom.

Arizona was one of the least restrictive states in the union
in terms of COVID, and after a brief lockdown, one of the first to
reopen in May. Mask-wearing and social distancing were generally lax, and mask mandates encountered fierce resistance
in a number of communities. At a protest in Scottsdale in June
2020, City Councilor Guy Phillips tore a mask from his face,
declaring "I can't breathe," seeming to mock the dying words of
George Floyd. Such sentiments fueled the broader view that the
liberals were hyping the threat of COVID in order to change the
system of the voting in ways that benefited the Biden campaign.

When the Fox Decision Desk called Arizona for Biden
at 11:20 p.m. on election night, Trump and the White House,
which had been ebullient after Florida went solidly for the president, were apoplectic. The early call for Arizona coming from
Fox made it much more difficult for the president to prema-
turely declare victory based on the early vote count, which had
been the core of his plan to raise doubt about the results and
challenge them in court. Despite pressure, including frantic

phone calls from Jared Kushner to Fox founder Rupert Murdoch, Fox stuck by the call.

Loftus, who has a grudging respect for the Fox Decision Desk, was disappointed. At the very least he believed the call was "about a week too early." But, in the end, the call was vindicated. Arizona went for Biden by around 10,000 votes, the first time it had voted for the Democratic candidate in a presidential election in nearly a quarter century. In the weeks after the election, Arizona saw a massive surge in COVID infections, eventually reaching a staggering rate of 122 per 100,000 people, far surpassing second-place California.

Like Charlie Loftus, Adrian Fontes grew up in Nogales, Arizona. He caught the democracy bug from his mother, a public school teacher, who encouraged him to watch *Schoolhouse Rock!* and many years later accompanied him on a trip to Athens where they toured the Parthenon. Fontes and his mother flew home to Phoenix on Monday, March 21, 2016. The next day, Arizonans went to the polls in primary elections to select their presidential candidates. Infused with the glow of his Athens trip, Fontes was disgusted as the voting lines backed up for hours turning the elections into what he described as a "holy disaster." Fontes decided then and there to run for Maricopa County Recorder, the top election official in one of the nation's largest and most sprawling districts.

A lawyer, Democratic Party activist, and Marine Corps veteran, Fontes had little political experience and thus no delusions about his chances against Helen Purcell, a Republican Party stalwart who had served as Maricopa County Recorder for more than three decades. But Purcell, eighty, had come under

116   attack and been hit with a flurry of lawsuits for mishandling
the primary elections. Purcell described her decision to vastly
reduce the number of polling stations as a cost-saving measure
but her critics called it a voter suppression strategy. Fontes's
ramshackle campaign looked like "the entire *Star Wars* crew on
the Millennium Falcon," so when he pulled off an upset victory
he acknowledged being unprepared for his new job. His prior-
ities were to simplify the voting process, make it more secure,
and enfranchise voters in a city "where Republicans had been
running the show and suppressing votes for a generation."

During his four years as Maricopa County Recorder, Fontes
improved voting technology and made the process more trans-
parent by giving voters live access to registration information. Most significantly, he expanded the voting rolls, adding
more than half a million new voters, a staggering increase of
more than 20 percent. While Fontes says his goal was to reach
all voters without regard to their political inclinations, his
efforts undoubtedly benefited Democrats, particularly because
they brought out of the shadows members of the county's large
Latino population, which skewed Democratic. That success,
not surprisingly, angered Republicans, who launched a series of
legal challenges.

In March 2020, with New York City in lockdown and pockets
of infection growing across the nation, Fontes was forced to reorganize the Maricopa County elections on the fly. He struggled
to obtain adequate PPE to wipe down polling stations and protect poll workers. He shifted polling from precinct-based to
polling-based, meaning that people would be permitted to vote
in polling places throughout the Phoenix area. He also sought to
expand the distribution of absentee ballots. Republicans were

able to obtain a last-minute injunction to block the effort. They
alleged that Fontes was exploiting the pandemic to illegally shift
voting patterns in a way that would benefit Democrats.

In order to insulate himself from accusations of partisan-
ship, Fontes sought to convey an air of neutrality and even-
handedness in his role as Maricopa County Recorder. The
problem, as Fontes saw it, was that he was locked in an increasingly partisan and bitter reelection battle with a formidable
Republican opponent, Stephen Richer. The fight was becoming
personal. One of the most visible signs was an election website entitled "Phony Fontes," which alleged that "Adrian Fontes
can't stop breaking the law." That claim was based on a 1989
incident in which Fontes, nineteen and troubled at the time,
had driven a scooter recklessly through the Arizona State University campus in Tempe, nearly knocking over several students, and then fled from a police officer who tried to arrest
him. That officer was Charles Loftus. Decades later, Loftus
remembered the arrest because "when I was booking him into
jail for the felony flight I noticed he was born in the same hospital as I was on the same day, down in Nogales. Our moms are
probably sitting there smoking Pall Malls in the delivery room,
back in the Sixties."

While Loftus was not directly involved in the campaign
against Fontes, other than donating a few hundred dollars to his
opponent, Richer, he had plenty of criticism. He accused Fontes
of election "shenanigans," including allowing non-citizens to
register to vote and using Dominion voting machines to tabulate
the election results. He alleged that dead people voted (presumably for Biden), a persistent but unsubstantiated claim specifically refuted by Arizona election officials. Such views widely

118   shared by Trump supporters in Arizona and later across the
        nation helped fuel the narrative—the Big Lie—that the entire
        presidential election was marred by fraud and that Trump had
        actually won.

        Because of the implications for the presidential race, Fon-
        tes's campaign was bombarded with false information that
        was amplified by the national media. On July 30, Trump him-
        self weighed in. He tweeted that universal mail-in voting, which
        Arizonans had relied on for decades, would result in the "most
        INACCURATE & FRAUDULENT Election in history." In the
        end, Fontes lost a close race—4,600 votes out of 2 million cast.
        Ironically, the narrow defeat, while personally painful, became
        the best way for Fontes to try to refute the allegations of fraud.
        "I lost fair and square," Fontes says. "I know because I ran the
        election."

        Chris Stirewalt, the Fox News politics editor who called Ari-
        zona for Biden and later left the network after receiving death
        threats, wrote, "The rebellion on the populist right against the
        results of the 2020 election was partly a cynical, knowing effort
        by political operators and their hype men in the media to steal
        an election or at least get rich trying. But it was also the tragic
        consequence of the informational malnourishment so badly
        afflicting the nation." He added, "The lie that Trump won the
        2020 election wasn't nearly as much aimed at the opposing
        party as it was at the news outlets that stated the obvious,
        incontrovertible fact."

        Loftus himself certainly wishes for a simpler time. "I got to
        meet Walter Cronkite," Loftus reminisced one day. "I just had
        to shake his hand. He wouldn't know me from the man on the
        moon. But he's long gone."

Nowadays, Loftus believes, "every media source is like research or statistics. You have to know who is doing it, why they are doing it, and who paid for it. There are fifty shades of gray with reporting events. The consumer must know the spin of the news agency, editor, or even the reporter." As a result, Loftus works hard each day to figure out what's going on in the world. But precisely because he doesn't trust the traditional media, he tends to be deeply influenced by the way that his community interprets and understands events. In the immediate aftermath of the January 6 Capitol riot, Loftus began receiving reports from the pro-Trump campus group that he advises at ASU that Antifa, a loose network of antifascist protesters, were behind much of the violence. "My guys have been pretty reliable," Loftus noted. "They wouldn't fabricate something." Loftus also found reports on Parler, the downloadable social media app favored by conservatives, that House Speaker Nancy Pelosi had demanded that an officer defending the Capitol fire on protester Ashli Babbitt as she tried to climb through a broken window and enter the Speaker's Lobby. "If that is true, she's culpable in some way," Loftus said. "Because she's giving him an order."

Experts who have sought to understand the ways in which people absorb disinformation and come to believe conspiracies all recognize the complexity of the problem, which defies easy solutions. For Joan Donovan, the social media companies must be compelled to recognize their civic responsibility. "We need some kind of mechanism and standard by which the larger platforms especially are going to ensure, that especially on life or death or civic integrity issues, that the truth shows up first," she noted. During the pandemic, social media platforms did move away from their traditional framework that prioritized

120   individual free expression, banning, blocking, and downgrading speech that undermined public health or could incite political violence. This included the decision by Facebook and Twitter to deplatform President Trump in the aftermath of the Capitol riot. Amazon meanwhile decided it would no longer host Parler on its server, a death knell for an app that had become a home to conspiracies and misinformation blocked on Facebook.

Such measures, while they may be justified during the pandemic and its aftermath to stem imminent harm, raise legitimate concerns about corporate censorship and free speech protections, which are at the heart of positive liberty. They are also immensely complex, often involving personal individual decisionmaking at the senior levels of the tech companies (i.e., deplatforming Trump), which are neither consistent nor scalable. Most experts therefore believe that the long-term solution should focus less on regulating content and more on regulating data, specifically the user tracking that social media companies do, which they then turn into advertising dollars. As Zeynep Tufekci noted in a seminal essay on the impact of social media published in the aftermath of the Trump election, "our cognitive universe isn't an echo chamber, but our social one is. . . . Belonging is stronger than facts." That is also true for Fox News and AM talk radio, which have built huge audiences united in a shared narrative of victimization. Some have suggested countering FOX's influence through a massive infusion of government funding to support local media. This is an idea that is explored in the next chapter.

Emily Bell, director of the Tow Center at Columbia Journalism School, believes that targeting the group dynamic is the only path forward. "So much is about community—community based belief," she notes. People trust media that reflect the values and perspective of the group of which they are a part. Thus, the way to create order out of the information chaos is to integrate communities that feel marginalized, misunderstood, and disenfranchised regardless of their perspective and experience. In other words, the infodemic cannot be overcome by tinkering with social media algorithms. It requires a political solution. Ultimately, the only way forward is to somehow find a way to bring the Charlie Loftuses of the world back into the information fold.

Right now Loftus is on the margins. For example, he is a strong supporter of the Maricopa County election recount that became a rallying point for Trump supporters. Using the online system implemented by Fontes, Loftus says he was able to determine that his mail-in ballot was never tabulated, nor was that of his wife or son. He does not trust for a second the state officials who say the votes were counted correctly and he does not believe the journalists who describe the recount as a misinformation operation intended to placate Trump supporters who believe the election was stolen.

But there is one conspiracy that Loftus does not believe. In early 2021, Loftus and his wife received their first Pfizer vaccines. Three weeks later, they got their second. They were thrilled with their new freedom. Loftus scoffs at the vaccine skeptics who believe in implanted microchips and secret side effects. He does, however, defend "their right to be stupid."

The Local Angle

The digital and social media revolutions decimated commercial advertising. Classified ad revenue dried up. Reporters were let go. Coverage of critical local issues disappeared. Some communities became news deserts. The pandemic tore like a whirlwind through these deserts, whipping up storms of confusion.

Study after study shows that citizens trust local news sources more than national outlets that might not even cover their issues and lives. Journalists who live and work among their audience have a better grasp of a community's needs. This chapter looks at the problems of the news industry globally and how COVD-19 has exacerbated them. In Mexico, the role of the local Tijuana weekly *Zeta* in documenting a COVID cover-up showed just how vital local journalism is, especially in times of crisis.

For forty years, since its founding in 1980, *Zeta* specialized in the coverage of local corruption and drug trafficking. It routinely exposed the ties between the cartels, the police, and government officials, which is what allowed the traffickers to operate with impunity. Two of its reporters have been murdered,

and the newspaper founder, Jesús Blancornelas, barely survived
a 1997 assassination attempt that killed his bodyguard.

When Blancornelas stepped down as editor of *Zeta* in early 2006, he left the newspaper in the hands of his protégé, Adela Navarro Bello, who today runs the weekly with Blancornelas's son, René Blanco. (Blancornelas died of natural causes in November of that year.) Navarro has maintained *Zeta*'s tradition of fierce independence and commitment to serve the community in covering the devastating COVID outbreak in Tijuana. She has refused to be cowed by attacks from state officials angry at the reporting. The problem, though, is that *Zeta* is running out of money.

Even before COVID emerged in Baja California, the state where Tijuana is located, *Zeta* and state officials were locked in a tense relationship. In November 2019, soon after new governor Jaime Bonilla assumed office, *Zeta* published a series of articles alleging that state officials had received kickbacks in exchange for government contracts. State Secretary Amador Rodríguez Lozano lashed out, alleging that Navarro had ulterior motives, including anger over a "supposed" corruption investigation into her personal partner. (Rodríguez Lozano later apologized, acknowledging his line of attack could be considered "machista.") Over the intervening weeks, officials sought to freeze out *Zeta* reporters and refused to include *Zeta* in a tour of a COVID hospital in the initial phase of the outbreak. All told, Navarro counted sixteen separate attacks from state officials between November and July. "It was an intense effort to discredit me as a person, *Zeta* as a publication, but also journalism in general," Navarro recalled. One state official even complained, "Fake news is everywhere."

The issue in Mexico, as in so many other countries we have examined throughout this book, was that because the government sought to downplay or deny the threat of the pandemic, reports from independent journalists, documenting the scale of the outbreak, represented a unique threat. Yet even among the COVID deniers, Mexico's president, Andrés Manuel López Obrador, stood out for his obstinance. In March 2020, as world leaders began to recognize the scope of the pandemic and the risk, López Obrador continued to hold rallies and wade into crowds to offer hugs and kisses to his supporters. When he was asked how he protected himself from infection, the president pulled two religious icons from his wallet, calling them "protective shields." It was not clear if he was joking.

Like other populist leaders who downplayed the disease—including Trump in the US and Bolsonaro in Brazil—López Obrador sought to dominate and overwhelm the information landscape. But AMLO (as he is known in Mexico, based on his initials) had a significant advantage, which was his daily morning press briefing, dubbed *la mañanera*, or "early riser." Every day at 7:00 a.m., López Obrador would stride to the lectern placed on a dais within the National Palace and for several hours he would talk. He would take questions, and parry with the journalists attending, often attacking and belittling those he deemed impertinent. The livestream was watched by millions of AMLO's supporters throughout Mexico, who use social media to amplify the president's discourse, attacking and drowning out all those who express disagreement. In this manner the president was able to shape the national narrative around COVID, which was that fears were overblown and the government response appropriate and measured. The president persisted with this story even as hospitals were overrun, oxygen became scarce, and Mexico surpassed India to briefly claim the third highest COVID death count after the United States and Brazil. Even after the president himself contracted COVID in early 2021, he refused to wear a mask.

As a member of AMLO's ruling MORENA Party, Baja California governor Bonilla adopted the same approach. While he lacked the president's magnetism and devoted followers, he used a daily livestream on Facebook to push back against reports that COVID-19 was spreading rapidly throughout the state. Dozens of journalists petitioned the governor to host a press conference, but he was unmoved.

Despite the threats, *Zeta* persisted in its reporting, relying on its networks of local contacts and its trust within the community to combat the governor's lies and distortions. The first COVID cases began to appear in Baja California in March 2020, at the beginning of a national lockdown, which was laxly observed. "From the beginning we realized that there was one set of the statistics that the government was giving each day, another that was coming from the Mexican Social Security Institute, and a third that was coming from the government laboratories," Navarro recalled. All three were different. And all three were wrong.

Zeta reporters pored through the records of the Tijuana Civil Registry, where all deaths are recorded. Their analysis revealed a spike in the deaths classified as "atypical pneumonia," which suggested that the government was undercounting the number of COVID deaths by 60 percent. They drove this home using a photo leaked to them by a doctor at Tijuana's General Hospital showing the whiteboard where deaths were recorded.

126   Case after case was classified not as COVID-related, but atyp-
       ical pneumonia. *Zeta*'s findings became national and interna-
       tional news, and eventually the Mexican government was forced
       to adjust its system for classifying cases.

       Meanwhile, families in Tijuana continued to reach out to
       Zeta reporters who they trusted to tell their stories of pain and
       loss, but also of negligence, incompetence, and indifference
       on the part of the authorities. Doctors got in touch to com-
       plain about the lack of personal protective gear, or of medicine.
       People were so upset that they began sending questions to the
       governor during his Facebook live session asking about the dis-
       parity with the state statistics. Indignant, Governor Bonilla
       claimed that *Zeta* was lying and that the only official informa-
       tion came from the state government.

       Recognizing the information vacuum, *Zeta* did all it could
       to get its reports to the people of Tijuana. It produced videos,
       used social media, and posted everything to its website. None of
       this made them a single cent. With print circulation dropping
       and advertising declining because of the pandemic, the paper
       found itself in crisis, compounded by the fact that thirteen of
       Zeta's fifty-five employees came down with COVID, and one
       needed to be hospitalized. The paper covered their wages and
       picked up their medical expenses.

       Over the years, *Zeta* has been buffeted by changes to the
       news industry that have negatively impacted local news orga-
       nizations in every part of the world. Their circulation dropped
       from a high of 50,000 a week in the 1990s, to 20,000 before the
       pandemic, before dipping another 20 percent after COVID hit.
       Advertising all but disappeared. Before the pandemic, Navarro
       had visited Tijuana businesses with a novel business strategy.

Relying on research suggesting that cities without local media have worse public administration and higher taxes, she had tried to convince local businesses that by advertising in *Zeta* they were not only supporting accountability but were making a savvy investment. The strategy worked, and *Zeta* was able to attract some new advertisers. But once the pandemic hit, the outreach stopped.

"Each week, I look over our invoices, and I see this one paid us, but this one didn't, and of course I think of the fifty-five families who depend on the weekly, but also the project of free expression and independent journalism that is very unusual in this country," Navarro reflected. "And I'm worried. I'm worried every day, every week. We have developed an enormous capacity to survive, and we do it week by week. In the late '90s, there was another dynamic within the society, the state, and a commitment to free expression. We could plan. Let's remodel the office. Let's buy cars. Let's put some money in the bank so we can pay for printing a year in advance. Now, we have no possibilities. We just survive week to week."

Zeta's independence is highly unusual for a local news organization in Mexico, but its exceptional coverage of COVID in Tijuana shows precisely what's at stake when local news outlets disappear. Around the world, the demise of local organizations, because of the financial challenges they face, opened the door for the misinformation, manipulation, and censorship that helped fuel the spread of the disease.

While local news has been declining for decades, the pandemic highlighted just how far the dual behemoths of Google and Facebook had corroded the pillars of a news industry built

128 on advertising revenue. In March 2020, people around the world wanted firsthand, accurate, and timely reporting on a disease they did not understand. If they relied on social media platforms, they didn't get it. There, a firehose of misinformation, self-serving opinion, and propaganda flooded the information landscape. As a result, it was easy for political leaders to use social media as a tool to overwhelm information networks and drive home their own narrative, as the case of Mexico shows. Some media scholars have termed this strategy "censorship through noise." It's not just a tool in the domestic arena. It's also a tool in the armory of the new censorship used by states like China and Russia, which have relied on social media–based propaganda to obscure the origins of the pandemic, cover up shortcomings in their own responses, and attack science.

In many countries readers value local news outlets more than the national press. Regional and local newspapers tend to be more trusted and are viewed as focused on the needs of the communities they serve. This is particularly true in countries with a federal system of government like Brazil, Germany, and the United States, according to the Reuters Institute's 2020 Digital News Report. Local news organizations also tend to be less polarized, as their business demands that they maximize readership within their own geographic region, rather than target people who share a political outlook but are dispersed across the nation.

As Navarro pointed out to potential *Zeta* advertisers, numerous academic and media industry studies show that towns and cities with strong local news outlets are better governed, suffer from less corruption, and enjoy higher voter turnout. As a Nieman Lab study put it: "Local newspapers are basically little machines that spit out healthier democracies." But many of these marvelous machines have been running on fumes.

While the decline of local news is a global phenomenon, most of the research and data is from the US, and to a lesser extent Europe. A close look at the US thus gives some sense of the challenges local media faces globally.

As noted, one of the biggest threats to local media everywhere is the loss of the advertising market. In the United States, Google and Facebook account for more than 60 percent of the digital ad industry, which is equivalent to $65 billion in revenue. Because of the siphoning off of these dollars, the United States has lost a quarter of its newspapers since 2005. Some 2,100 titles have folded, leaving at least 1,800 communities without a local newspaper, according to research from the Hussman School of Journalism and Media at the University of North Carolina (UNC). Online news sites and television have filled some of the gaps, but at least 1,300 US localities are without any local news coverage whatsoever.

As publishers struggled to adapt to the loss of their lucrative lock on the local advertising market, asset strippers and hedge funds swooped in looking for bargains among ailing publishing companies. They wrung profit out of them through consolidation or by running them into the ground, selling off assets, and cutting staff. Many of the 6,700 titles that have survived in the United States have been hollowed out. Industry analysts call them "ghost newspapers." With the arrival of COVID and mass population lockdowns, newspaper revenues plunged even further. Penny Abernathy, the Knight Chair in Journalism and Digital Media Economics at UNC, described the pandemic as "an extinction-level event" when it comes to local news.

In fact, more than ninety US newsrooms disappeared in the year following the outbreak of the virus. With advertising already overwhelmingly going to the large platforms that provide cheap, highly targeted advertising at scale, COVID brought an economic downturn that hit local communities hard. Retailers cut spending on digital display advertising, throttling local news portals. Search and social advertising revenue, which does not go to news publishers in any case, fared better.

Within weeks of the first lockdowns, an estimated 37,000 employees of US news media companies had been fired, furloughed, or had their pay cut, according to the *New York Times.* The pattern was repeated in several Western countries. More than 2,000 staff across the UK's national and regional press were furloughed or had their salaries cut shortly after the start of the outbreak, the UK *Press Gazette* found. Globally, advertising revenue fell 11.8 percent in 2020 according to a Thomson Reuters Foundation study. All in all, the pandemic cost the media worldwide about $20 billion in income.

Advertising revenue to media outlets plummeted even as demand for their reporting about the virus soared. Many outlets logged record numbers of visitors to their sites but were unable to monetize this fully and fared badly unless they already had a strong subscription funding model. Some of the bigger and better resourced titles in the US and Europe temporarily brought their COVID coverage out from behind paywalls as a public service.

Among the top six US public companies that own more than three hundred dailies, advertising revenue plunged 42 percent in the second quarter in 2020 compared with the same quarter a year earlier and circulation revenue dropped 8 percent, according to a Pew Research Center analysis.

The pandemic also accelerated a trend of local audiences moving toward a limited number of large national and international titles and television for their news. This added to the financial woes of local news providers. One of the reasons local outlets find it difficult to gain a foothold in the world of digital media is that they account for a tiny fraction of the time people in the United States, for example, spend online with news and media. According to the survey group Comscore, all news and information providers combined account for some 4 percent of time spent online, and all local news providers together account for just half of 1 percent.

The Pew analysis showed that Americans initially flocked to television for news of COVID, and the ad revenues of the traditionally trusted three main broadcast networks' nightly news shows rose 11 percent. On cable, Fox News Channel showed a 41 percent jump in ad revenue. Over the same period CNN and MSNBC both saw a surge in viewership but their ad revenue dropped 14 percent and 27 percent respectively as marketers pulled their ad spend or delayed campaigns until later in the year. As we saw in chapter 5, Fox viewership, particularly of opinion hosts who downplayed the threat of the disease and echoed President Trump's denialism, also corresponded with higher rates of COVID infection.

Europeans, too, turned on the television to try to make sense of the crisis. The audience for the evening news bulletins of public service broadcasters doubled in eighteen European countries, including Germany, France, Spain, Italy, and the UK,

132   which were also some of the hardest hit nations in the world. The evening news shows, whose audience normally skews older, saw a 20 percent jump in young viewers. Daily viewing rose 14 percent on average.

Ironically, many of these same broadcasters had been under political and commercial pressure to cut spending for years, including among editorial staff. Now they had to honor this show of public trust and need for firsthand reporting by scrambling depleted resources to keep up with a spreading plague that had much of western Europe locked down like a war zone. To add to their woes, the shutdown of much of the economy pushed advertising spending off a cliff. Those broadcasters that were funded wholly or in part by commercials saw their revenue plunge by an average of 50 percent in a matter of weeks.

Audiences also turned to legacy media, but the COVID bump in readership and subscription revenue went mainly to the big national or international brands like the *New York Times*, the *Washington Post*, *Le Monde* in France, and *The Guardian* in the UK. Readers looking for national news in such media were well served, but localization of content, particularly in big countries with federal systems, was limited.

The wasting away of local news outlets had created a vacuum that platforms peddling misinformation or lies were quick to fill. Around the world, social media—fueled political polarization and misinformation engendered what the World Health Organization called an "infodemic," as described in the introduction and chapter 5. In many countries, misleading information and conspiracy theories sparked heated public debates about the severity of the disease, death rates, and the efficacy of preventative measures like social distancing and mask-wearing.

National media then amplified these debates. Social media platforms, with their opaque algorithms tailoring content to keep
users online and in front of ads, fanned the flames. In their business model, fear and anger breed engagement. Locked down
at home for months on end, people were already spending an
average of 50 percent more time on screens and so were easy
prey in their self-selected echo chambers for outrage-inducing
opinion and clickbait, as well as government-orchestrated misinformation campaigns.

In the era of YouTube and Facebook, journalists are no
longer the privileged gatekeepers of information. In any event,
nearly half the people online do not get their information from
recognized news sites but from social media, friends, family,
and interest groups both online and offline. Tech companies
pledged to clamp down on inaccurate COVID information but
their platforms were awash in it.

Citizens trying to wade through this morass of misinformation needed a local press that served not only as a conduit
of accurate news but as a watchdog. The loss of local newspapers' shoe-leather reporting meant less scrutiny of officials and
their actions (or sometimes inactions) in fighting the disease,
the kind of reporting *Zeta* routinely carried out. Social media is
full of content, but Google and Facebook don't send news crews
into hospitals' COVID intensive-care units or pay reporters to
wait for hours outside of local government offices and legisla-
tures in the hope of buttonholing an official or lawmaker.

Despite the financial carnage, it is print publishers who still
employ the bulk of reporters in the US and many other leading
media markets and invest in news gathering. The US Bureau of
Labor statistics in 2016 showed print employing the majority of

134   reporting staff, with broadcasters accounting for about 25 percent and online media 10 percent. In the UK, the corresponding
figures were 69 percent, 10 percent, and just 1 percent from digital media, according to Rasmus Kleis Nielsen, head of the Reuters Institute for the Study of Journalism at the University of
Oxford.

Local news outlets and the staff or freelancers they employ
are often the source of investigations and breaking news that
broadcasters and digital sites then pick up and amplify. "When
the real information people were seeking was about closures in
their area, school closures, mask mandates, essential workers,
local, state, and national relief funds, they turned to local news
providers," said Rebecca Frank, vice president of research with
the News Media Alliance, which represents about 2,000 newspapers in the US. "News providers have never been more valu-
able to consumers and yet these news companies, because of the
way that advertising has changed . . . have been doing that work
for less compensation."

As noted, data about the decline of independent local
news and its impact on coverage of the pandemic is still limited outside of the industrial democracies. But initial reports
are worrying. Brazil, which as we have seen in chapter 3 has been
inundated with misinformation from the top down, is riddled
with news deserts, defined as towns without any news sources,
and semi-deserts, communities that have one or maybe two
news outlets, according to the Institute for the Development of
Journalism (Projor). This means that many Brazilians in these
areas, which are mainly rural, either got no information or
sometimes misleading or biased information from outlets that
lack the resources to do critical reporting.

"The problems of the national press tend to be more acute in local journalism, which often depends on less-specialized sources and is more exposed to the influence of politicians and businessmen," said Marcelo Träsel, president of the Brazilian Association of Investigative Journalism.

Meanwhile, lockdowns in parts of sub-Saharan Africa dried up an already dwindling revenue stream for many media companies. Journalists lost jobs or took pay cuts as local businesses slashed advertising in newspapers and on FM radio, which is still a vital source of information across a continent where more than 60 percent of people do not have internet access. Audiences seeking an alternative to state-run outlets for COVID news turned to commercial and community news organizations, but many of those organizations struggled to meet the challenge with fewer reporters and less money.

Governments also cut back on official advertising, an important income source for newspapers. Those media houses that have managed the transition to digital in more mature markets like Nigeria, Kenya, and South Africa also took huge hits.

"First, it is important to stress that most news organizations during the COVID-19 age are churning out more content online than ever before. Many news organizations on the continent have transitioned to digital platforms in the past five months—much more than at any other time in history," said Ntibinyane Ntibinyane, a veteran editor and media expert in Botswana. "The problem, however, is that they have not figured out how to make money online. They are clueless. News outlets, in particular newspapers, are running out of money and time during this crisis. This forced transition will lead to the deaths of many newspapers on the continent."

The pandemic showed that in a world in which information has become a denationalized, shared global resource, safeguarding democracy and ensuring accountability require robust local media. How can be this achieved?

One way is to get Big Tech to share the wealth. Publishers have been lobbying governments and regulators to push Big Tech to pay for news for years. The US has been reluctant to regulate Silicon Valley and is certainly wary of forcing platforms to pay publishers. But the pandemic has changed public attitudes toward tech giants by throwing into relief just how polluted the information landscape has become. Calls for everything from breaking up Big Tech under antitrust provisions in the US to heavier taxes and market regulation in Europe have grown.

COVID has also rekindled the debate in many western European countries, Canada, and Australia over who should pay for news. Google and Facebook, already sensitive about their image as news free-riders, had begun subsidizing small groups of journalists, news websites, and journalism institutions even before the pandemic. But the amounts are tiny compared with the companies' overall revenues and the sheer scale of news desertification.

In France, Google agreed in January 2021 to start paying some publishers, and the following month it extended its Google News Showcase initiative to the UK with the promise of paying some British news providers. All news industry eyes, however, were on Australia where the government strong-armed tech platforms into paying publishers in what could become a precedent for other governments. The companies lobbied hard against the law, the News Media and Digital Platforms

Mandatory Bargaining Code, which required them to negotiate licensing agreements with publishers for the news articles that appear on Google's search and Facebook's feed.

Google threatened to pull search from Australia and Facebook briefly cut Australian news outlets from its services in an unprecedented move. In the end, both companies cut separate deals estimated to be worth a total of $47 million to Australian publishers. Just how much of that will prop up small local news organizations is not clear. Australia's news industry is highly concentrated: Rupert Murdoch's News Corp and local media giants Seven West and Nine Entertainment are likely the biggest beneficiaries.

COVID has also hastened the demise of much of the ad-model old media and accelerated the move to paid subscriptions with content behind a paywall. Some outlets have morphed into nonprofits dependent on private philanthropy; others in Europe and Canada have accepted government subsidies. Marquee titles like the *New York Times* and the *Washington Post* have strengthened their subscriber base and so, too, have some European papers like *Dagens Nyheter* in Sweden, *NRC* in the Netherlands, and France's *Le Monde*. New digital entrants *El Diario* in Spain, *Malaysiakini* in Malaysia, and *Denník N* in Slovakia have also seen a surge in readers. But overall, the losers from the revolution in the media business and the depredations of COVID still outnumber the winners.

"The many losers will be those communities who will be less well-served in the future because they aren't among the groups that news organizations are able to build a sustainable business around," says the Reuters Institute's Nielsen. "And these

138   groups I fear will primarily be in poor countries. They will be
in poor areas and they will be poor people in big rich cities who
will be even less well-served by journalism and news media in
the future than they've been so far."

However, the pandemic has helped turn the tide in the
debate for public funding of the media in the United States.
Some conservatives have long argued that the government has
no business supporting the media: they conflate subsidies with
the loss of editorial independence, the fostering of political bias,
or the danger of government censorship. This ignores a long
history of federal government support for news distribution.
The founders of the US republic understood the importance of
an informed electorate and began subsidizing postal rates for
newspapers and periodicals in 1792. Congress also funds public
television and radio and regulates broadcast, wire, and cable
media through the Federal Communications Commission.

"It is striking that the only private business mentioned in
the US Constitution—and accorded rights by it—is the press;
that reflects the understanding of its vital role in our democracy," said Harvard Law School professor Martha Minow. She
argues that, far from discouraging state support for the press,
the Constitution encourages it.

"As the press suffers from economic, technological, and
political challenges, there is at least a moral imperative for col-
lective, including government, action to strengthen the news
ecosystem and the press generally. And although it is a reach, I
think the case can be made for a government duty to act."

Some US lawmakers have already heeded the call. They have
introduced a slate of proposals for saving local news ranging

from direct government subsidies to news organizations to
loosening antitrust legislation that curbs the newspaper industry's bargaining power.

Such ideas are not viewed as revolutionary outside of the
US. State funding of media is commonplace in many liberal
democracies, especially those with a tradition of public service broadcasting. Many of these broadcasters, as we see in this
chapter and in chapter 3, became valued news sources during
the pandemic.

Canada has an income tax credit for local news subscribers,
and France, which already provides $1.2 billion a year in direct
subsidies to newspapers, introduced a similar income tax credit
as COVID took hold.

"Increasingly, local news groups are coalescing around a
novel idea: give Americans $250 to buy local news subscriptions
or make a donation to local news nonprofit organizations," said
Steve Waldman, president of Report for America, which places
journalists into local newsrooms. "Under this approach, it
would be consumers, not government officials, deciding who to
support. It is strictly nonpartisan and nonideological." Minow
believes in a blend of state and private support. "There is no
silver bullet or single action that will help, but a combination
of direct and indirect subsidies, enforcement of copyright and
antitrust laws, and treating as responsible actors the internet
platforms that cannibalize and undermine legacy media would
help; national, state, and local governments, as well as philanthropy and ordinary people all have vital roles to play," she said.

While the scale of the problem is enormous, there are also
projects to support local news on a global level, particularly

140   in countries where press freedom is under attack. The International Fund for Public Interest Media aims to pump both state and private funds into reviving local outlets in low- and middle-income countries. Over the years, nations and private foundations have doled out tens of thousands of grants to individual news ventures and journalists with mixed success. Some governments have used media development aid principally to project soft power. The $1 billion International Fund would represent an independent, coordinated attempt at scale to build resilient public interest media, which could not only inform underserved communities but hold their leaders to account. Of course having well-supported and robust local news doesn't matter if no one reads it. Here is where the tech platforms must be brought in as partners to develop and deploy algorithms that provide users with reliable and accurate information from local news sources based on their location.

The challenge in rebuilding local news is not just the money, it's the data. As noted, in the developing world there is little research on the decline of local media. But anecdotal evidence suggests much has already been lost and that the pandemic accelerated the negative trends. In some regions of Mexico, for example, drug-related violence and economic hardship have created "silent zones," with almost no media, no news, and no accountability. For forty years, *Zeta* has been able to make a go of it in Tijuana. But the shift to the digital economy coupled with the COVID recession has brought the paper to the brink of economic collapse. The demise of *Zeta* would give even freer rein to demagogues using social media to manipulate public opinion and advance their political agendas. "If you are not aligned with the COVID statistics that the president is giving out, then you

are his enemy and you are a liar," Navarro noted. "The president,
just like Governor Bonilla, believes he possesses the truth."

The goal of Bonilla, López Obrador, and increasingly of so many political leaders in Mexico and around the world is to use social media to pump out endless information, much of it false or misleading, to overwhelm the news ecosystem and drown out critics. Former Trump strategist Steve Bannon cynically called it "flood the zone with shit." It's a modern censorship strategy that has worked exceedingly well, sometimes with deadly consequences in those places where local news organizations have disappeared or have shrunk to the point where they no longer have the resources to fight back.

The Meaning
of Freedom

On December 28, 2020, authorities in Shanghai wheeled Zhang Zhan into a courtroom because she was too weak to stand. Facing a sentence of five years for the uniquely Chinese crime of "picking quarrels and provoking trouble" as well as disseminating "large amounts" of fake news, Zhang had gone on a hunger strike to protest her unjust treatment. Prison authorities resorted to forced feeding, binding Zhang's hands so she could not remove the feeding tube.

Like Chen Qiushi, Zhang was a lawyer turned information activist who had traveled to Wuhan in February 2020 to document what was happening in the city. She had a background in insurance and finance, and had moved to Shanghai from her native Xianyang in Shaanxi Province in order to pursue professional opportunities. While Chen took pride in his role as a lawyer and sought to a certain extent to work within the system, Zhang had the heart of a dissident. In September 2019, she was arrested by Shanghai police after she held up an umbrella with

the message: "End Socialism, CCP step down," referring to the
Chinese Communist Party. She was detained for sixty-five days
and subjected to forced psychological examination, which she
resisted through hunger strikes.

Zhang arrived in Wuhan in early February, right around the
time of Chen Qiushi's arrest. One of the first videos she posted
from the city called for his release. She also mourned the death
of Li Wenliang, the ophthalmologist whose warnings about
COVID-19 had been suppressed and whose death from the disease in February 2020 had set off waves of public grief. "If Chinese citizens still don't have freedom of expression, then we are
all Li Wenliang," Zhang declared.

Perhaps because Zhang did not have Chen's visibility
or social media following, she was able to operate in the city
until May 14, when she was finally picked up by the authorities. While Chen Qiushi has been quietly released to home custody, Chinese authorities seemed to want to make an example of
Zhang. In part this may have been a response to her defiance, but
it may have also been intended as a message to China and the
world. Zhang's trial was covered not only in the Chinese media,
but also in the international press. Her persecution was widely
denounced outside of China. Such appeals did not influence the
Chinese government or the judges who condemned her to four
years in prison, a pitiless sentence that seemed intended to dis-
suade anyone from following in Zhang's footsteps.

By December 2020, the Chinese government felt confi-
dent not only that it had contained the spread of COVID-19 in
China, but also that it had reasserted control over the domestic
information space. These efforts had come at some cost. China

144   has invested a fortune in new measures to monitor and control online speech, while jailing those like Zhang who could not be censored through other means.

Meanwhile, China continued to assert control over Hong Kong, seeking to close a back door for independent information about political developments on the mainland. Only a few weeks before Zhang's sentence, publisher and democracy activist Jimmy Lai was charged with violating the newly enacted National Security Law, an offense that carried a possible life sentence.

Globally, China sought to shape perceptions of how COVID-19 originated and became a pandemic. It used its influence within the WHO to delay or suppress information that was politically damaging to China and sought to control any effort to investigate the origins of the disease, particularly the possibility that it had been caused by a lab leak. A WHO delegation that was finally able to visit Wuhan in January 2021 seemed to go out of its way to leave unchallenged the unsubstantiated Chinese government theory that the virus had originated outside the country and had arrived in China via a shipment of frozen food.

Zhang's sentencing closed the door on the notion briefly asserted in the early days of the outbreak that China's failure to contain the disease, and its suppression of essential and life-saving information, could force a Chernobyl-like public reckoning. To the contrary, China emerged from the pandemic stronger and more assertive, and arguably with greater influence and leverage over international institutions, including those that nurture and sustain democracy at the global level. Smothering state surveillance, already a fact of life in China, had also been strengthened even as China had successfully avoided the worst ravages of a terrible disease. Now through Zhang's harsh and highly public sentencing, China seemed to be asking a provocative question. Because of the country's success in combating COVID following the initial outbreak in Wuhan—a success achieved by deploying the full resources of the author- itarian state—people were free to go about their lives so long as they did not challenge government authority.

Was this a bargain that the world would be willing to accept?

A month after Zhang's sentencing, in January 2021, vaccines began to roll out in a handful of countries around the world, offering an alternative to China's false dichotomy. The most effective vaccines, developed by Western companies thanks largely to a huge infusion of resources from the US and other democratic nations, promised a future in which people could reclaim their freedom: no more mask mandates; quarantines; or lockdowns. By the late summer, despite their enormous success, the promise of a mask-free future had been tempered by the spread of the Delta variant, as well as the staggering inequality of vaccine distribution at a global level. In some Western coun- tries, notably the US, vaccine hesitancy combined with active resistance to vaccine mandates had stalled inoculation drives.

The global debate over freedom and COVID-19 as exempli- fied by Zhang and the vaccine rollout is impossible to untangle without returning to Isaiah Berlin's formulation of positive and negative liberty. By censoring Zhang in the most brutal and direct way, China was sending a message that the people of China could have greater negative freedom (freedom from government-imposed lockdowns and mask mandates) only if they surrendered any positive freedom, including their already extremely limited ability to criticize the Communist regime. Many authoritarian countries around the world offered a variation of this trade-off, though their case was less compelling since it was based not on success in containing the disease but on covering up and denying its impacts. This was generally accomplished through censorship.

The counterargument that the democratic world failed to make was one based on positive liberty: we can preserve our ability to participate in a political system that protects essential rights if we trust our political leaders to limit our negative freedom in ways that are prudent and necessary to contain the pandemic. But the trust, understandably, wasn't there. In the populist-led democracies described in chapter 3, it had been severely compromised by a style of scorched-earth, winner-take-all politics that led to polarization and paralysis. A genuine and informed public debate was undermined by the use of new censorship strategies that included drowning out critics and harassing them into silence. And of course while a successful vaccination campaign might end mask mandates, it would do nothing to address the enormous rollback of positive liberty that had accumulated during the pandemic year.

In October 2020, Freedom House, the Washington, DC—based research and advocacy organization, released a report entitled "Democracy Under Lockdown," which concluded, "Since the coronavirus outbreak began, the condition of democracy and human rights has deteriorated in eighty countries around the world." The report, based on a survey of nearly four hundred global experts, found that governments routinely used the

pandemic as a "justification to grant themselves special powers
beyond what is reasonably necessary to protect public health."
As noted in chapter 2, ninety-one countries, nearly half of all
those in the research, imposed restrictions on the media, in
other words new censorship measures. Freedom House's annual
Freedom in the World survey, released in March 2021, was even
more bleak. For the fifteenth consecutive year, the report noted,
freedom had declined around the world. "As COVID-19 spread
during the year, governments across the democratic spectrum repeatedly resorted to excessive surveillance, discrimi-
natory restrictions on freedoms like movement and assembly,
and arbitrary or violent enforcement of such restrictions by
police and nonstate actors," the report noted, adding, "[T]he
COVID-19 pandemic has triggered a shift in norms and the
adoption of problematic legislation that will be challenging to
reverse after the virus has been contained."

The report highlighted a number of countries around
the world, from Indonesia to the Philippines, to Hungary and
Poland, to El Salvador, Egypt, and Algeria, all of which exploited
the pandemic to introduce repressive laws or generally curtail
freedom. But the most disappointing result by far was India,
which for reasons described in chapter 3 moved from the free
to partly free classification. "Under Modi, India appears to have
abandoned its potential to serve as a global democratic leader,
elevating narrow Hindu nationalist interests at the expense of
its founding values of inclusion and equal rights for all," the
report concluded.

Because of India's enormous population, the country's shift
into the partly free category meant that, according to Freedom
House's data, only 20 percent of the world's population now live

148   in a country classified as free. This is a decline from 60 percent in 2006, when, according to political sociologist Larry Diamond, "the democratic recession began." Diamond attributes the recession to a variety of factors, including the rise of elected autocrats who use the legitimacy conferred upon them at the ballot box to undermine and weaken democratic institutions. He also notes the rise of Chinese and Russian "sharp power," which he defines as a coercive strategy short of military means that works in the shadows to corrupt institutions. "The malign influence of the regime in China, the world's most populous dictatorship, was especially profound in 2020," the Freedom House report noted.

A second independent research project on the impact of the pandemic on democracy reached a similar conclusion. Two-thirds of all countries around the world logged violations relating to democratic standards during 2020, according to data compiled for the Sweden-based Varieties of Democracy research project (V-Dem). As with Freedom House, the V-Dem analysis revealed a continuation of long-term antidemocratic trends. "The level of democracy enjoyed by the average global citizen in 2020 is down to levels last found around 1990," V-Dem noted. The rise of "electoral autocracy" combined with "closed autocracies" meant that 68 percent of the world's population lives under an autocratic regime. By contrast, the number of liberal democracies declined over the past decade from forty-one to thirty-two, and today account for only 14 percent of the world's population.

Outside of India, much of the decline was attributable to countries that inhabited a gray zone, variously described as

illiberal, managed, or hybrid regimes. These are the places
where the COVID-related regression is most troubling and will
be most difficult to reverse. In the Philippines, for example,
the country's populist president, Rodrigo Duterte, exploited
the pandemic to accelerate a power grab that Maria Ressa, the
embattled editor of the renowned news website Rappler, called
the death knell for Philippine democracy.

In March 2020, soon after COVID hit the archipelago,
Duterte's loyal legislature granted him sweeping emergency
powers, including the power to requisition public transportation for health care workers, to take control of private util-
ities, telecoms, and businesses, and to force hotels and other
properties to house medical workers or serve as quarantine
facilities. Another provision criminalized spreading "false
information," which was defined so broadly as to encompass
anything the regime did not like. In July 2021 Duterte signed
into law The Philippine Anti-Terrorism Act, which allows for
arrest without a warrant, lengthens the period a suspect can be
detained without charge, and provides for wiretapping for up
to ninety days. It established an Anti-Terror Council that can
define terrorism however it wishes and tag anyone who challenges authority as suspicious without judicial oversight. "Do
not intimidate the government. Do not challenge the government. You will lose," Duterte warned.

Studies carried out by a range of researchers suggest there
is no correlation between a country's system of government and
its effectiveness in fighting COVID-19. Some leading democracies fared well, others poorly. Some clearly benefited from government interventions; others may have just gotten lucky. Some

150   enacted mandates and imposed restrictions that were legally
       sound; others used persuasion to convince citizens to change
       their behavior.

       Among the high performing democracies were South Korea,
       which was able to deploy rapid testing and contract tracing early
       on; Japan and Taiwan, which adopted near universal mask-
       wearing among other interventions; and Canada, Australia, and
       New Zealand, which used aggressive quarantine measures and
       restrictions on movement to contain the first wave of the dis-
       ease (though Australia and New Zealand, with their popula-
       tions largely unvaccinated, were forced to lock down much of the
       country for months to contain the spread of the Delta variant).

       Europe's record was much more mixed. Several countries in
       Europe were devastated by the first wave; others were impacted
       more modestly. Throughout continental Europe, there were
       abuses, some serious, including harassment of journalists by
       police and other officials in Spain, Italy, and France. The lock-
       downs, restrictions on movement and assembly, sparked some
       legal challenges and protest, most notably in Germany, which
       has seen a rise of right-wing activity grounded in part in a lib-
       ertarian critique of the Merkel government. On the EU's more
       authoritarian periphery, abuses were far more severe. The most
       egregious case was Hungary, where Prime Minister Viktor
       Orbán, who had already eviscerated civil society and gutted the
       country's independent media, used his party's control over Par-
       liament to secure legislation allowing him to rule by decree.
       "Let's face it, the decisionmaking process is more simplistic
       and faster in an authoritarian regime," Sophie Wilmès, the
       former prime minister of Belgium who oversaw the country's
       COVID response, acknowledged. "The challenge in a democratic

country is to fight the pandemic but at the same time abiding by
the rule of law and not infringing on human rights."

Under international law, governments have the right to impose temporary restrictions or even suspend certain rights in response to threats to public health. To do so legally, they must first declare a state of emergency, and show why severe restrictions are necessary. Any restrictions imposed must be non-discriminatory and time-limited. Because such restrictions represent a breach of international human rights obligations to which governments are bound, such measures are classified as "derogations" and should be registered with the UN or the appropriate regional body. But of the eighty-three countries that restricted fundamental democratic rights during the pandemic, only forty-four declared a state of emergency. Not one country registered a derogation with the UN related to violations of free speech.

Censorship has been a defining feature of the COVID-19 pandemic, from the initial outbreak in Wuhan, China, throughout the authoritarian world, and in many leading democracies, where the tactic was not to suppress dissenting views but to drown them out. This wave of global censorship was driven by a near universal desire to downplay the threat of COVID and cover up government failures. Censorship undermined the global response to the pandemic, obscuring the origins of the disease and stifling an informed public debate about what Isaiah Berlin identified as the central question of politics: government obedience and coercion.

In China and many authoritarian countries, censorship is a critical feature of state authority because it allows the

152   government to control or if necessary crush the political debate that is the most essential feature of positive liberty. As noted, there was little correlation between a country's political system and efficacy in fighting the disease, with some authoritarian countries faring well and others faring poorly. Thus, the defense of positive liberty cannot be based on efficacy in fighting the pandemic. It must be based on a belief in the inherent value of freedom. The impact of censorship, and the way it was used to expand state power and erode essential rights and liberties in authoritarian countries, is well documented and straightforward, as the case of China makes clear. But what is the relationship between censorship, rights, and the pandemic in the democratic world?

To answer that question, it's necessary to recognize the way in which thinking about public health and government authority has evolved in the last century. In fact, the authority of governments to coerce individual behavior to protect public health has long been ratified in domestic and international law, beginning with *Jacobson v. Commonwealth of Massachusetts*, a 1905 US Supreme Court decision affirming the legality of mandatory vaccination programs. "The liberty secured by the Constitution of the United States to every person within its jurisdiction does not import an absolute right in each person to be, at all times and in all circumstances, wholly freed from restraint," wrote Justice John Marshall Harlan in upholding the right of Massachusetts to require the vaccination of a local pastor named Henning Jacobson. Jacobson had resisted being vaccinated against smallpox because he argued the vaccine itself posed a risk to his health. That ruling has been widely affirmed in legal challenges to mandates related to the COVID vaccine in the United States.

But just because governments have the moral and legal authority to compel behavior to protect public health does not mean it is expedient for them to do so. While Jacobson made clear that the government *could* take coercive action, in the decades following the decision, US public policy, at least as it related to infectious diseases, moved away from coercion and toward an emphasis on persuasion.

The reasons were twofold. First, as science and modern hygiene reduced the risk of widespread contagion, governments were less willing to use coercive measures even if they had the authority to do so. Secondly, a Progressive Era belief in the power of public education, coupled with technological innovation that improved mass communications, led governments to rely on persuasion to convince the public to accept vaccination programs or shift their behaviors in ways that benefited the communities of which they were a part.

The AIDS epidemic of the 1980s and 1990s introduced a new framework for the debate, which was human rights. A recognition that the population most impacted by AIDS/HIV, gay men, would fiercely resist any effort to coerce personal behavior in the name of protecting public health led authorities to eventually conclude that such strategies would not only be futile but also counterproductive to the extent they would increase mistrust among the targeted population. Instead, public health authorities focused on education and persuasion as a means of changing behavior among the impacted group and allaying fears born of ignorance on the part of the general population. Some activists and academics put forth a broader argument, which was that restrictions on civil liberties and human rights always undermine public health. However, international law permits

154   the abrogation of certain human rights to protect public welfare when a state of emergency has been lawfully declared, as noted earlier.

In October 2020, *Foreign Affairs* published an analysis, which, citing newly available data, concluded that at the onset of a new pandemic, at a time when there was no effective treatment or immunity, "the only way for government to effectively protect citizens from one another is by convincing them to take the necessary measures to protect themselves. Especially in free societies, the success of that effort depends on the trust between the government and its people."

Certainly, democracies should produce a higher level of trust in their citizens and should therefore be better positioned to use persuasion to change behavior while preserving human rights and civil liberties. Trust is made actionable through effective communication that empowers citizens to make informed decisions. Censorship is thus the most essential betrayal of public trust.

In the United States and other leading democracies, the debate over censorship and freedom was turned on its head, leading to a highly distorted understanding of what was at stake. Because censorship was accomplished by drowning out rather than suppressing alternative viewpoints, removing content, deplatforming Trump from Facebook and Twitter, or blocking YouTube posts from Bolsonaro made it more difficult for them to engage in censorship through noise, though it hardly ended the practice.

On the other hand, empowering tech platforms to more aggressively regulate content and ban political leaders is a devil's bargain, expeditious in the moment but hardly a sustainable

or scalable solution to the problem of information chaos. It
also has obvious implications for political discourse and public
debate.

Political leaders also in many instances managed to manipulate the debate over freedom to focus exclusively on negative liberty, *freedom from* government-imposed lockdowns and
mask mandates. By doing so, they turned the spotlight away
from the threats to positive liberty, the *freedom to* participate in
the political process and hold political leaders accountable. This
is exactly the opposite of how the question of freedom should
be understood. In a pandemic, we must surrender negative liberty to the state in order to preserve public health, while fighting
ever harder for positive liberty, the ability to debate government
action, and use the political system to hold leaders accountable. An example of why this is critical comes from Norway, as
described in chapter 4. There, a small group of citizens pushed
back against their government after it hastily introduced a contact tracing app that compromised privacy. The government
upheld their right to be free of excessive surveillance, dropping
the app and switching to a less intrusive alternative.

Such examples are exceedingly rare in the context of the
pandemic. Instead, the pandemic allowed governments through
censorship to consolidate and strengthen state power in nearly
every corner of the globe. In China, this was made explicit
through the arrest of bloggers like Chen Qiushi and the jailing
of Zhang Zhan. Iran, Russia, Egypt, and Nicaragua used censorship to cover up the scope of the outbreak while asserting new
government authority. In Brazil, the United States, and India,
not to mention the Philippines, governments systematically
undermined the essential institutions of democracy in order

156   to advance a false narrative about the government's COVID response. Misinformation promulgated by governments themselves was a tool of censorship, used to undermine debate and confuse the public. Social media was a useful tool employed by governments and political leaders for this purpose.

The focus of citizens in the post-pandemic world must be to fight against the consolidation of state power and the corrosive influence of governments over the information space. The consequences were clear during the pandemic, but censorship undermines political decisionmaking every day in every corner of the globe. Throughout the pandemic, many people felt as if they were drowning in information. In fact, they were being censored.

Fighting against censorship in all its forms is the only way to ensure that the voices of people everywhere are heard. It is some of the most essential work of the post-COVID era. People can only retain autonomy over their own existence if they are able to participate in the process through which state power is exercised and laws and policies are formulated. That freedom, in turn, is what compels us to obey restrictions and mandates imposed to protect health. Censorship has broken the link between positive and negative liberty. It's a link that must be repaired.

This book chronicles one of the most remarkable years in human history and describes events that took place in nearly every corner of the globe. Over decades as journalists and press freedom defenders, the authors have lived, worked, and traveled in dozens of countries, developing local knowledge, contacts, and relationships that we drew on in our reporting and writing *The Infodemic*. We also built a remarkable network of journalists and experts who carried out the firsthand reporting, conducted many of the interviews, and provided analysis. We are grateful to Iris Hu, Paula Ramón, Madeleine Wattenbarger, Uriel García, and Heidi Ghavidel-Syooki. We are especially grateful to Jean-Paul Marthoz in Brussels.

While based in the United States, Courtney Vinopal played an essential role through her research on human rights, democracy, and press freedom. She also reviewed the manuscript and helped compile the endnotes.

The authors also relied on the amazing experts of the Committee to Protect Journalists and their documentation of the COVID crackdown, from Azerbaijan to Zimbabwe. Among the CPJ colleagues who provided detailed feedback and support are Elana Beiser, Madeline Earp, Steve Butler, Jan-Albert Hootsen, Yeganeh Rezaian, Gulnoza Said, and Sherif Mansour. Andrés Fernández Carrasco prepared research documenting press freedom incidents in the first few months of the COVID outbreak.

We also imposed on the goodwill of our friends, many of them busy writers themselves, to read chapters and provide feedback. These included Sandy Rowe, David Kaye, Patricia

158   Campos Mello, Eric Siblin, Andrew Paxman, Julie Orringer, Maureen Linker, and Ann Cooper. Their insights improved the manuscript immensely. The authors are responsible for any errors.

Our agent, Stephanie Steiker, helped us conceive of this project and found the perfect home. Columbia Global Reports is a unique publisher that has made an enormous contribution to human understanding. The authors are proud to be associated with such an effort, and grateful to the director, Nick Lemann; publisher, Camille McDuffie; and editor, Jimmy So.

Finally, the authors recognize that *The Infodemic* would never have been written without the love and support of our families. Joel would like to express his everlasting gratitude to his daughters, Ruby and Lola, and his wife, Ingrid Abramovitch. In the case of Rob, he's indebted to his children, Daniel, Thomas, and Susannah; daughter-in-law, Michelle; and partner, Alisa.

This is a book about the terrible toll of a disease, not in terms of human health, but rather to democracy, human rights, and press freedom around the world. The authors are grateful to the journalists who documented the pandemic, putting their lives on the line to tell terrible but humanizing stories and to make sense of something that not long ago seemed unimaginable. We celebrate their work, and pay homage to their courage.

INTRODUCTION

In *Four Essays on Liberty*, Isaiah Berlin, one of the preeminent political thinkers of the twentieth century, celebrates freedom, rejects determinism, and makes the case for pluralism as an organizing principle for modern societies.

In *Apollo's Arrow: The Profound and Enduring Impact of Coronavirus on the Way We Live*, physician and sociologist Nicholas A. Christakis writes about where the novel coronavirus came from and where it has taken us.

In *The Plague Year*, Lawrence Wright tells the story of how COVID-19 gained a foothold in the United States and how the failures of government and the health officials allowed the disease to spread.

Nightmare Scenario: Inside the Trump Administration's Response to the Pandemic That Changed History by *Washington Post* reporters Yasmeen Abutaleb and Damian Paletta offers an insider account of decisionmaking in the Trump White House.

CHAPTER ONE

Wuhan writer Fang Fang won praise in China for a detailed personal chronicle of life under lockdown during the initial outbreak, originally published on Weibo, a Chinese social media app. The accolades turned to scorn after her posts were compiled in a book, *Wuhan Diary*, which became an international bestseller and cast a critical light on the conduct of Chinese officials.

CHAPTER TWO

In *This Is Not Propaganda*, Peter Pomerantsev shows how the enemies of freedom have weaponized social media and turned truth on its head.

In *How Democracies Die*, Harvard professors Steven Levitsky and Daniel Ziblatt show how the gradual undermining of vital institutions such as the judiciary and the press have stifled democracies from 1930s Europe to modern-day Turkey, Venezuela, and Hungary.

CHAPTER THREE

Brazilian journalist Patrícia Campos Mello in *A Máquina do Ódio* shows the ways in which the Bolsonaro government, from the president on down, has

160   used social media to attack critics, divide the country, and advance their
       own political project (in Portuguese).

       Anne's Applebaum's *Twilight of Democracy* is a collection of her essays,
       originally published in *The Atlantic*, including her analysis of political ori-
       gins of the COVID pandemic.

       ## CHAPTER FOUR

       *The Age of Surveillance Capitalism: The Fight for a Human Future at the New
       Frontier of Power* by Shoshana Zuboff examines how the threat to personal
       privacy has shifted from a totalitarian Big Brother state to a ubiquitous dig-
       ital architecture: a "Big Other" of commercial interests that monetize our
       data.

       In *We Have Been Harmonised: Life in China's Surveillance State*, German jour-
       nalist Kai Strittmatter draws on his more than twenty years as a correspon-
       dent in Beijing to dissect how the Communist Party of China exerts near
       total political and social control over 1.4 billion people.

       ## CHAPTER FIVE

       Alan Rusbridger, former *Guardian* editor and digital media trailblazer, dis-
       mantles the modern information ecosystem in *Breaking News*.

       CNN media reporter Brian Stelter has spent years building up sources
       within Fox News. *Hoax: Donald Trump, Fox News, and the Dangerous Distor-
       tion of Truth* is the closest thing to an insider account.

       George Packer has distinguished himself as one of the most important
       chroniclers of American inequality and in *Last Best Hope* he describes how
       the deep divisions in American society informed the politics of the COVID
       year.

       ## CHAPTER SIX

       Born in Mexico and raised in California and Texas, Alfredo Corhado
       describes his life between two worlds as well as his life as a journalist in
       Midnight in Mexico.

       Penelope Muse Abernathy tracks the decline of the for-profit business
       model that has sustained local journalism in the United States for more

than two hundred years in *The Expanding News Desert* and highlights the damage this has done to our ability to make sense of our immediate world.

Drawing on her experience as former chief editor of the *Buffalo News* and now media columnist for the *Washington Post*, Margaret Sullivan chronicles the painful decline of local media across the US in *Ghosting the News*.

CHAPTER SEVEN

In *Surviving Autocracy*, Masha Gessen offers a blistering takedown of Trumpian politics drawn from their knowledge and understanding of the forces that created Putin's Russia.

David Kaye, the former UN Special Rapporteur for Freedom of Expression, argues in *Speech Police* that online content moderation must be grounded in human rights principles.

Journalists John Micklethwait and Adrian Woodbridge analyze the problems of governance and leadership that the pandemic has highlighted and offer some solutions for the post-COVID world in *The Wake-Up Call*.

One of the first books published on the impact of the coronavirus, Fareed Zakaria's *Ten Lessons for a Post-Pandemic World* offers a perspicacious analysis of the political origins and consequences of the disease that still resonates two years on.

INTRODUCTION

13   **"The question of obedience and coercion":** Isaiah Berlin, *Liberty*, edited by Henry Hardy (Oxford University Press, 2002), p. 168. Berlin sought to make the argument that Western liberal democracy could protect and nurture freedom by placing limits on government authority while creating safeguards to protect the rights of citizens to participate in the political process. But he acknowledged a lack of correlation, noting that those who live in totalitarian states may have a greater degree of negative freedom than those living in democracies. This paradox has become more pronounced in the post–Cold War era in which a new generation of populist authoritarians have retained power by delivering economic growth and respecting personal autonomy outside the political realm. They focus their energy less on policing personal behavior, but on suppressing political organizing and controlling the information to which citizens have access.

14   **"the trouble is that we usually don't think hard enough about all that's actually required":** Kwame Anthony Appiah, "The True Face of Freedom Wears a Mask," *Wall Street Journal*, August 8, 2020.

14   **"For a sense of common cause to appear":** Masha Gessen, "Life, Liberty, and the Pursuit of Spitting on Other People," *New Yorker*, May 26, 2020.

CHAPTER ONE

17   **Chen Qiushi:** was in Chinese state custody during the period that this chapter was written. He was released at some point in the fall of 2020 and was believed to be living with his parents under strict supervision in early 2021. Because of the risk of contacting Chen, the account of his background and activities in Hong Kong and Wuhan is drawn entirely from open sources, including his numerous YouTube videos, which are still available online. These were compiled, summarized, and translated for the authors by researcher Iris Hu.

18   **making him the most popular "legal" personality on the entire platform:** Chen made this claim in his YouTube bio.

18   Additional background on Chen: During a speech to university students in Changchun, Jilin Province, Chen recalled that he had only studied law to please his mother and that his true passion was journalism: Qi Wang, "'I'm a speaker' runner-up Chen Qiushi Ji staged a talk show," *Jida News*, April 1, 2015. While Chen did not discuss his marital status

specifically, he did note while traveling through Wuhan, "I saw many elders not wearing masks. We should just nag them to wear masks just like they nag us to get married."

18   Background on Hong Kong protests: Tripti Lahiri, "A refresher course on Hong Kong's 2014 Umbrella Movement," Quartz, September 27, 2019. See also Daniel Victor, "Why Are People Protesting in Hong Kong?" New York Times, November 13, 2019.

20   **Chen used his first video on August 17:** https://www.youtube .com/watch?v=tULDO9ZMil4.

21   **"Under the circumstances where information is so confusing":** https://youtu.be /tULDO9ZMil4.

22   **"90 percent of the two million":** https://www.youtube .com/watch?v=tULDO9ZMil4.

23   **"I came here to foster the communication between the two sides":** https://www.youtube.com /watch?v=tULDO9ZMil4.

23   **"It is my responsibility as a citizen journalist":** https:// www.youtube.com/watch?v =CuToaalqPo4.

23   For background on Wei Guixian and early days of COVID: Jeremy Page, Wenxin Fan, and Natasha Khan, "How It All Started: China's Early Coronavirus

Missteps," Wall Street Journal, March 6, 2020. See also Bethany Allen-Ebrahimian, "Timeline: The Early Days of China's Coronavirus Outbreak and Cover-Up," Axios, March 18, 2020.

24   **They blocked an international investigation into the origins:** Selam Gebrekidan et al., "In Hunt for Virus Source, W.H.O. Let China Take Charge," New York Times, November 2, 2020.

25   **"But I, Chen Qiushi, am here":** https://www.youtube.com /watch?v=CuToaalqPo4.

25   **China is often classified as one of the most censored countries in the world:** "10 Most Censored Countries," CPJ, September 10, 2019.

25   Background on Wang Chen speech: Joel Simon, The New Censorship (Columbia University Press, August 2019), pp. 96–97.

27   **While China banned the use of uncertified Virtual Private Networks (VPNs) in 2018:** Benjamin Haas, "China Moves to Block Internet VPNs from 2018," The Guardian, July 11, 2017.

27   **China is the world's leading jailer of journalists:** "Record Number of Journalists Jailed Worldwide," CPJ, December 15, 2020.

28   **"Although I was blocked on the internet in China for reporting**

164   **on the events in Hong Kong":** https://www.youtube.com/watch ?v=CuToaalqPo4.

29   **twenty-seven-minute monologue:** Jane Li, "Wuhan Virus: Chinese Citizen Journalist Reports from Quarantine Zone," Quartz interview, February 6, 2020.

30   **unable to reach Chen:** Derek Hawkins, "Chen Qiushi, Citizen Journalist Who Covered Coronavirus Outbreak, Disappears in Wuhan," *Washington Post*, February 9, 2020.

31   **Fang Fang:** *Wuhan Diary: Dispatches from a Quarantined City* (HarperCollins, June 2020).

31   **Ai Weiwei assembled a powerful documentary:** *Coronation*, August 20, 2020.

31   **Fang Bin:** Vivian Wang, "They Documented the Coronavirus Crisis in Wuhan. Then They Vanished," *New York Times*, February 14, 2020.

31   **Li Zehua:** "Li Zehua: Journalist Who 'Disappeared' After Wuhan Chase Reappears," BBC, April 23, 2020.

31   **Zhang Zhan:** Vivian Wang, "She Chronicled China's Crisis. Now She Is Accused of Spreading Lies," *New York Times*, December 25, 2020, and Helen Davidson, "Citizen Journalist Facing Jail in China for Wuhan Covid Reporting," *The*

Guardian, November 16, 2020. Her story will be featured in chapter 7, focusing on threats to freedom.

31   **2008 Sichuan earthquake:** "Deadly Earthquake Doesn't Shake China's Internet Censors," *Wired*, May 23, 2008.

31   **2011 high-speed train crash in Wenzhou:** Chris Buckley, "China Train Crash Censorship Scorned on Internet," Reuters, July 31, 2011.

32   **On March 10, President Xi:** Chieu Luu and Yuki Tsang, "Chinese President Xi Jinping Visits Wuhan for First Time Since Start of Coronavirus Outbreak," *South China Morning Post*, March 10, 2020.

32   **global propaganda networks:** Anne Applebaum, "The Rest of the World Is Laughing at Trump," *The Atlantic*, May 3, 2020. See also Erika Kinetz, "Anatomy of a Conspiracy: With COVID, China Took Leading Role," Associated Press investigation, February 15, 2021, on how the country peddled falsehoods about the virus.

33   **A survey released in June 2020:** Polling by the Alliance of Democracies Foundation and Dalia Research, covered in Reuters, "China's Response to COVID-19 Better Than U.S.'s, Global Poll Finds," June 15, 2020.

33   **China's response to the coronavirus outbreak:** "'If the

Chinese Press Were Free, the Coronavirus Might Not Be a Pandemic,' Argues RSF," Reporters Without Borders, March 24, 2020.

33   **a visa war:** Steven Butler, "Prospects Bleak for Recovery of US Media Presence in China," CPJ, July 20, 2020. On February 19, 2020, the US designated five Chinese media organizations, including Xinhua, as "foreign missions" controlled by the Chinese government. It had long been a point of contention among US officials that hundreds of Chinese "journalists" were granted visas to work in the US when their real role was to support Chinese state propaganda or to directly inform the Chinese government rather than report the news, a kind of low-level spying. But the timing of the decision to designate Chinese media as foreign missions suggested it was less of an attempt to address this legitimate concern than a ham-handed effort by the Trump administration to seek leverage in the ongoing trade dispute with Beijing. Within weeks, China expelled three actual reporters working for the *Wall Street Journal*, claiming they were taking action in response to an offensive headline in the *Journal*'s opinion section. On March 2, after the US limited the number of visas available to Chinese journalists, China revoked visas for thirteen journalists for US media organizations, including the

Washington Post and the *New York Times*. Between February 2020 and the end of the year, at least sixteen international reporters were expelled from China.

33   **noted Paul Mozur:** Michael Barbaro, "Kicked Out of China," *The Daily*, April 16, 2020.

35   **Xu Xiaodong announced via video:** https://www.youtube.com /watch?v=9K3Qo01GGAM. In September 2021, a year after Xu Xiaodong first announced that Chen had been released from custody but was under state supervision, Chen made an appearance in a YouTube video posted by Xu. Chen was circumspect about his circumstances, saying that he suffered from depression and had taken up boxing. Over the next few weeks, Chen made several attempts to get on various social media platforms, but his accounts were blocked and his posts deleted. In November, Chen managed to tweet out a video message describing how boxing had brought him a sense of peace and purpose. But Chen had not lost his spunk. In another video posted on Twitter, he noted "watch until the end and you will know my situation." The video panned quickly to three police officers sitting outside of the boxing gym, who were clearly monitoring Chen's every move. Chen also tweeted out his support for Zhang Zhan, who had undertaken a hunger strike to

166 protest her unjust imprisonment. "I truly hope she receives humane care," Chen tweeted. "If her life is in danger, we are all guilty." See https://youtu.be/my8nzYX2ODA ?t=476 https://twitter.com /chenqiushi404/status/145576213 8136416257 (also RFI report, quoted Chen's Tweet) and https://www .youtube.com/watch?v=gIeO4np SeXY&t=1s.

CHAPTER TWO

37 **A trend toward authoritarianism that the US watchdog Freedom House said had been underway for the past fifteen years**: Sarah Repucci and Amy Slipowitz, "Democracy Under Siege," Freedom House, March 2021.

38 Russia's response to COVID: Jeffrey Mankoff, William Heerdt, and Timothy Kostelancik, "Russia's Response to Covid-19," Center for Strategic and International Studies, April 10, 2020; Ann Cooper, "How Russian Media Reported the Coronavirus Pandemic," Nieman Reports, April 11, 2020; Ann Cooper, "Conveying Truth: Independent Media in Putin's Russia," Shorenstein Center, August 10, 2020.

39 **He promised them bonuses, which some complained were never fully paid out:** Maria Antonova, "Russian Medics Ask Where Putin's Virus Bonuses Went," *Moscow Times*, May 14, 2020.

40 **Police accused Tatyana Voltskaya:** "Russian Journalists Investigated, Fined over COVID-19 Reporting," CPJ, June 16, 2020.

40 **Milashina wrote in the independent newspaper** *Novaya Gazeta*: "Chechen Leader Threatens Journalist Elena Milashina over COVID-19 Reporting," CPJ, April 15, 2020.

40 **Dmitry Belyakov, a paramedic in the city of Zheleznodorozhny near Moscow:** "Russia, Explained #32," *Novaya Gazeta*, April 29, 2020. See also "'All the Hospitals Are Full': Russia's Health-Care System Scrambles as COVID-19 Cases Rise," RFE/RL, April 29, 2020.

41 **By July 2020, only 23 percent of Russians said they trusted Putin:** "Government Approval and Confidence in Politicians," The Levada Center, July 29, 2020. The survey was conducted on July 24–25, 2020, on a representative sample of the Russian population of 1,617 people aged eighteen and over. The study was conducted via telephone interviews (CATI) on a random two-basic sample (RDD) of mobile and landline phone numbers. The statistical error does not exceed 2.4 percent. The distribution of answers is given as a percentage of the total number of respondents.

41 **Russia authorized its Sputnik V vaccine in August 2020:** Olga

Dobrovidova, "Russia's COVID-19 Defense May Depend on Mystery Vaccine from Former Bioweapons Lab—But Does It Work?" *Science*, April 6, 2021.

41   **only 16 percent of Russia's 146 million people had been vaccinated:** "Russia's COVID Death Toll Hits Record High for Fifth Day," Al Jazeera, July 4, 2021.

41   **showed excess deaths in Russia to be a staggering 494,610:** "Tracking Covid-19 Excess Deaths Across Countries," *The Economist*, May 11, 2021.

41   **authorities arrested Navalny's relatives and supporters:** "Navalny's Family Members, Allies Detained for Virus Violations at Protests," *Moscow Times*, January 28, 2021.

42   **packing more than 80,000 people into the capital's Luzhniki Stadium:** Robert Coalson, "Dying for a Dose of Putin? With Sagging Ratings, Russian President Holds Mask-Optional Rally," RFE/FL, March 19, 2021.

42   **"Our situation is better than in many other countries":** Jake Rudnitsky, "Russian Covid Cases Surge Over 10,000 for First Time Since March," Bloomberg News Wire, June 9, 2021.

43   **a thriving black market in forged vaccination certificates:** Evan Gershkovich, "Russian Vaccine Skeptics Rush to Buy Fake Covid Jab Certificates," *Moscow Times*, June 25, 2021.

43   **"Love in the Time of COVID-19":** "Nicaragua: Reckless COVID-19 Response," Human Rights Watch, April 10, 2020.

43   **When Ortega resurfaced on April 15:** Ismael Lopez, "Nicaraguan President Reappears After More Than a Month Out of Public Eye," Reuters, April 15, 2020.

43   Nicaragua's response to COVID: Andy A. Pearson, Andrea M. Prado, and Forrest D. Colburn, "Nicaragua's Surprising Response to COVID-19." *Journal of Global Health*, June 27, 2020.

44   **he asserted without evidence:** Wilfredo Miranda Aburto, "Nicaragua's 'Express Burials' Raise Fears Ortega Is Hiding True Scale of Pandemic," *The Guardian*, May 19, 2020. See also Ismael López Ocampo and Mary Beth Sheridan, "The President Has Vanished; His Wife, the VP, Says the Coronavirus Isn't a Problem. Nicaragua Declines to Confront a Pandemic," *Washington Post,* April 12, 2020.

44   Nicaragua's COVID statistics: "Resultados 30 de abril al 06 de mayo, 2020," Citizen Observatory for COVID-19, May 8, 2020.

44   **Some 700 health care workers wrote Ortega demanding action:** "Second statement by

168   independent health professionals on the current situation of COVID-19 in Nicaragua," Progressive Alliance, May 28, 2020. See also Carrie Kahn, "Citizens Work to Expose COVID's Real Toll in Nicaragua as Leaders Claim Success," NPR, May 12, 2021.

44   ten public health workers . . . were fired: "Nicaragua, Doctors Fired for COVID Comment," Human Rights Watch, June 23, 2020.

45   Nicaragua is the second poorest country in the hemisphere after Haiti: "Poorest Countries in North America 2021," World Population Review.

45   Congress passed a "foreign agents" law: "Nicaragua Passes Controversial 'Foreign Agent' Law," AFP, October 16, 2020.

45   cybercrime law: "Nicaragua Approves 'Cybercrimes' Law, Alarming Rights Groups," Associated Press, October 27, 2020.

45   Law for the Defense of the People's Rights: "Nicaragua Passes Law to Sideline Adversaries in 2021 Election," Reuters, December 21, 2020.

45   Cristiana Chamorro: "Nicaragua Presidential Aspirant Charged, Will Face Trial," Associated Press, September 2, 2021.

46   At an International Workers' Day rally on May 1: Kahn, "Citizens Work to Expose COVID's Real Toll in Nicaragua as Leaders Claim Success," NPR, May 12, 2021.

46   Sources for the section on Iran include these Farsi news sites: **Hamshahrionline** is the online version of *Hamshahri* newspaper, which is owned by the Tehran Municipality. It previously had members of the Khamenei family as well as members of the current Majlis Speaker Mohammad Baqer Qalibaf network on its board of directors. **Khabaronline** is affiliated with former Majlis Speaker Ali Larijani. **Mojnews** is a conservative outlet. Its board of directors includes former Isfahan MP and conservative politician Hamidreza Fouladgar, conservative politician Mostafa Mir-Salim (current MP and member of the Expediency Council), and MP Mohammad Reza Pour Ebrahimi. **Jahansanat.ir** is the online version of the moderate Jahan Sanat newspaper, which was temporarily banned on August 10, 2020, for publishing an interview with a member of the COVID-19 Task Force, Mohammad-Reza Mahboubfar, in which he said the Health Ministry statistics on COVID deaths and infections were one-twentieth of the real numbers.

46   Iran's commercial links with the West were restricted by US sanctions, but its ties with China,

its biggest trading partner: The European Commission reported in November 2020 that China, the United Arab Emirates, and the EU are now Iran's main trading partners, accounting for 19.5 percent, 16.8 percent, and 16.3 percent, respectively. The EU used to be the first trading partner of Iran before the current sanctions regime.

47   **The protests proved to be the most widespread political unrest in the Republic's history:** Farnaz Fassihi and Rick Gladstone, "With Brutal Crackdown, Iran Is Convulsed by Worst Unrest in 40 Years," *New York Times*, December 1, 2019.

47   **Social media and messaging apps such as Telegram were abuzz:** See "Are the First Cases of Coronavirus from Qom City?" Khabar Online, February 19, 2020.

48   **"holy-shrine-licker":** Rozina Sini and Armen Shahbazian, "Coronavirus: Iran Holy-Shrine-Lickers Face Prison," BBC, March 3, 2020.

48   **stormed the courtyards of both sites in protest:** "Hard-line Shiites Storm Iran Shrines Closed over Coronavirus," Associated Press, March 17, 2020.

48   **suspension of flights to and from China on January 31:** Original source: https://www.magiran.com /article/4026675. Sharq outed Mahan's Air on March 11. The Sharq exposé also pointed out that while Mahan had released photos of flight crew in PPE, flight crew, who spoke to the newspaper on condition of anonymity, revealed no one in the flights had actually been given masks or gloves or any other form of protective gear and that none of the flight crew observed a fourteen-day quarantine upon returning from international flights. They also informed the paper that at least one Mahan employee had died after contracting the virus. See also "Coronavirus by Air: The Spread of Covid-19 in the Middle East," BBC, May 5, 2020; "Iran Guard's Mahan Air continued flights to China amid coronavirus outbreak: report," Arab News, March 19, 2020; "How an Iranian Airline Tied to Terrorism Likely Spread the Virus (and Lied About It)," *Foreign Policy*, March 30, 2020.

49   **IRGC belatedly acknowledged:** "Iran Plane Crash: Ukrainian Jet Was 'Unintentionally' Shot Down," BBC, January 11, 2020.

49   **It has banned Twitter, Facebook, YouTube, and Telegram:** See "Iran" in "10 Most Censored Countries," CPJ, 2019.

49   **They uploaded videos:** Regime media outlets published photographs, which opponents said appeared to have been

170 photoshopped or taken from misleading angles, to show large crowds participating in the state-organized event. However, some Iranians countered by posting videos to discredit the official narrative. For instance, a video taken by a skydiver and posted to Twitter on the revolution anniversary shows an overhead shot of Azadi (Freedom) Square and the sparse crowd attending the event. Another similar video shows only a dozen people chanting "Allah Akbar" and walking down Jomhori (Republic) Street. Some social media accounts created a mashup of videos taken by netizens from different cities, which also show small crowds of people—many of whom were clergy—turning out for the anniversary of the revolution. Parts of these videos show teenage students, who are typically forced to participate in such events, in school uniform subverting the call-and-response of the leader of the march. Instead of repeating the chant "Trump the thug has gone mad" and " Death to America," they shout "shut the fuck up." Videos of anti-regime protests posted to Twitter and YouTube were reviewed by Iran researcher Heidi Ghavidel-Syooki.

49 **Turnout for the parliamentary election was the lowest in the Republic's history:** "Iran Elections: Record Low Turnout but Hardliners Set for Win," BBC, February 23, 2020.

50 **"one of the enemy's plots to bring our country into closure by spreading panic":** Tom O'Connor, "Iran Warns of 'Enemy Plots' to Spread Coronavirus Fear as U.S. Questions Official Statements," *Newsweek*, February 25, 2020.

50 **announced dozens of arrests:** The commander of the Iranian Cyber Police, Vahid Majid, told Afkar News that police were monitoring online activity and would prosecute anyone publishing material that contained "rumors or lies which disturbed public opinion or increased anxiety in society." See "Arrest of 24 People and Summoning and Warning of 118," *Afkar News*, February 26, 2020.

50 **Mostafa Jalalifakhr:** https://www.instagram.com/p/B8GElYeJbDb/?utm_source=ig_web_copy_link.

51 **nurse at Qom's Kamkar Hospital posted a video journal:** On March 9, 2020, Cleric Ali Mozaffari, who is the head of the Qom courts, announced that a nurse who had given false statistics about the number of deaths in Qom had been arrested and detained for three days as his actions had "disturbed public opinion," according to a report by Persian language news site the Young Journalists Club. The news site Iran International said the nurse worked at Qom's Kamkar Hospital.

52 **finally confirmed that two patients had died from the virus:** "Rumors of Seeing the Coronavirus in Qom Were Denied," *Moj News*, February 1, 2020. See also "The Ministry of Health confirmed the death of two people due to the coronavirus in Qom," Transportation Industry News Network, February 19, 2020.

52 **member of parliament Ahmad Amirabadi Farahani announced that fifty people had died:** "Coronavirus: Iran's Deputy Health Minister Tests Positive as Outbreak Worsens," BBC, February 25, 2020.

52 **said if the toll were even a quarter of that, he would resign:** Golnaz Esfandiari, "Coronavirus Cover-Up? Iranian Officials Deny That Qom Death Toll at 50," Radio Free Europe/Radio Liberty, February 24, 2020.

52 **rescinded permission for the charity Médecins sans Frontières:** "MSF 'Deeply Surprised' That Iranian Authorities Put a Stop to Our COVID-19 Response," MSF, March 25, 2020.

53 **forced to do a second interview:** "The Nurse of Qazvin Hospital Tells the Truth of the Story of 51 Days Away from Family + Video," ILNA.

54 **By the end of 2020, Iran had recorded some 1.2 million cases:** Worldometer tracking website, updated continuously.

54 **As early as August 9, Mohammad Reza Mahboobfar:** "Analysis of Fluctuations in Corona Casualty Statistics in Recent Days in an Interview with Mohammad Reza Mahboobfar: Do Not Trust Government Statistics," *Jahan Sanat*, August 9, 2020.

54 **The paper was banned for twenty days by the Press Supervisory Board:** "Jahan-e-Sanat Newspaper Was Banned After an Interview with a Member of the Corona Counter-terrorism Headquarters," Radio Farda, August 10, 2020.

55 **3,600 people had been arrested for spreading false information about the pandemic:** "Iran Says 3,600 Arrested for Spreading Coronavirus-Related Rumors," RFE/RL, April 29, 2020.

56 **Egypt has blocked some six hundred websites covering news and politics since 2017:** "Egypt: Events of 2019," Human Rights Watch.

56 **authorities arrested el-Balshy's brother, Kamal:** "Egyptian security forces detain brother of Darb editor Khaled el-Balshy," CPJ, October 13, 2020.

56 **since the 2018 expulsion of *Times* of London correspondent Bel Trew:** She was detained after interviewing a relative of a man who died on a migrant boat to Europe. No immediate official explanation

was given for her detention and no charges were brought. She was driven to the airport by police and made to take a flight to London. See Richard Spencer, "Times Reporter Bel Trew Expelled as Egypt Tightens Media Grip," *The Times*, March 24, 2018.

56   Ruth Michaelson, *The Guardian*'s Cairo correspondent: Michaelson cited a report by scientists from the University of Toronto, which based its assessment on a preprint looking at the spread of the virus from Iran: Ashleigh R. Tuite et al., "Estimation of COVID-2019 Burden and Potential for International Dissemination of Infection from Iran," pulled from medRxiv database, February 25, 2020.

56   Egypt had reported just 166 infections and 4 deaths in a country of 100 million people: "Egypt Targets Guardian, NYT Journalists over Coronavirus Reports," Al Jazeera, March 18, 2020. See also Al-Masry Al-Youm, "Health Minister: Egypt's Reported COVID-19 Cases Represent One-Tenth of Actual Cases," *Egypt Independent*, January 5, 2021.

57   Tourism employs about one in ten Egyptians: "Egypt: Tourism in the Economy," OECD iLibrary, 2020.

58   journalist pleaded in a Facebook Live post: M. ElHaies, "Mohamed Monir's Death of COVID-19 Is a Warning Sign for Journalists Held in Egypt's Prisons," CPJ, August 6, 2020.

58   doctor in the Mediterranean port city of Alexandria was picked up: "Egypt: Health Care Workers Forced to Make Impossible Choice Between 'Death or Jail,'" Amnesty International, June 18, 2020.

59   string of detentions of medical professionals: "Release Detained Doctors and Medical Members, and Honor Their Martyrs," the Arabic Network for Human Rights Information, November 15, 2020.

59   resigned in protest at a lack of proper equipment: "Release Detained Doctors and Medical Members, and Honor Their Martyrs."

59   Ahmed Safwat, who merely described in a Facebook post a situation that Egyptians could see for themselves: Owen Dyer, "Covid-19: At Least Eight Doctors in Egypt Arrested for Criticising Government Response," *British Medical Journal*, July 15, 2020; "Release Detained Doctors and Medical Members, and Honor Their Martyrs."

59   while six doctors died in South Africa over the same

period, Egypt recorded 117 deaths: Dyer, "Covid-19: At Least Eight Doctors in Egypt Arrested for Criticising Government Response."

60 **With just 140,000 cases and 7,400 deaths by the end of 2020:** Worldometer tracking website.

60 **Freedom House estimates:** Sarah Repucci and Amy Slipowitz, "Democracy Under Siege: Freedom in the World 2021," Freedom House, February, 25, 2021.

CHAPTER THREE

62 **Luiz Henrique Mandetta:** Interviewed by Zoom, December 14, 2020. When Mandetta was tapped to be Bolsonaro's health minister in 2018, he was under investigation for alleged fraud, influence peddling, and undeclared campaign donations. Mandetta denied the allegations. See "Governo Bolsonaro: Quem é Luiz Henrique Mandetta, que será ministro da Saúde," BBC, November 20, 2018.

65 **declare the coronavirus outbreak a global health emergency:** The WHO declined to declare COVID a global health emergency on January 23, 2020, but did so a week later on January 30. See Andrew Joseph, "Who Declines to Declare Coronavirus a Global Health Emergency," Stat News, January 23, 2020, and Sarah Boseley, "Who Declares Coronavirus a Global Health Emergency," *The Guardian,* January 30, 2020.

66 **Mar-a-Lago on Saturday, March 7:** Peter Baker and Katie Rogers, "On a Saturday Night in Florida, a Presidential Party Became a Coronavirus Hot Zone," *New York Times,* March 14, 2020. See also Christine Stapleton, "Maskless at Mar-a-Lago: Partying, Cozy Photo Ops and Political Huddles Amid Pandemic," *Palm Beach Post,* January 8, 2021, and Emily Goodin, "Kimberly Guilfoyle Celebrates Her 50th at Lavish Mar-a-Lago Birthday Bash as Trump Loudly Sings Happy Birthday Before the Former Fox News Presenter Shows Off Her Dance Moves with Beau Don Jr.," *Daily Mail,* March 8, 2020. Following the COVID outbreak, the Trump campaign sent an email to guests who attended the Mar-a-Lago event informing guests who wanted to "learn more about the COVID-19 and ways to keep you, your family, and your community safe . . . to visit the CDC's dedicated website." These were the same guidelines that Trump himself had disparaged and ignored.

67 **began touting the benefits of the antimalarial drug hydroxychloroquine:** On Bolsonaro and hydroxychloroquine,

174   see "Brazil's Bolsonaro Hails Hydroxychloroquine Even as He Fights Coronavirus," *New York Times*, July 8, 2020, and "Why Is Brazil's Bolsonaro Peddling Hydroxychloroquine?" *The World*, July 22, 2020.

70   **What Modi demanded from the country's media was obeisance:** "PM Interacts with Print Media Journalists and Stakeholders," official website, March 24, 2020.

70   Background on press freedom in India: Kunal Majumder, "Mission Journal: Journalists in India's Uttar Pradesh Say Threat of Attack or Prosecution Looms Large," CPJ, April 23, 2020. See also "How Science in India Became a 'Political Weapon' Under Modi," *New York Times*, September 14, 2021; Siddharth Varadarajan, "In India, a Pandemic of Prejudice and Repression," *New York Times*, April 21, 2020; Sameer Yasir and Kai Schultz, "India Rounds Up Critics Under Shadow of Virus Crisis, Activists Say," *New York Times*, July 19, 2020.

70   **took legal action against Siddharth Varadarajan:** Varadarajan, "In India, a Pandemic of Prejudice and Repression." See also Siddharth Varadarajan, "Pegasus Project: How Phones of Journalists, Ministers, Activists May Have Been Used to Spy on Them," The Wire, July 18, 2021.

72   **Thousands of COVID-related fatalities were reported each day:** "Mass Funeral Pyres Reflect India's COVID Crisis," AP: April 26, 2020; "India Covid: Dozens of Bodies Wash Up on Banks of Ganges River," BBC, May 20, 2020.

72   **In Bergamo:** Jason Horowitz, "The Lost Days That Made Bergamo a Coronavirus Tragedy," *New York Times*, November 29, 2020. See also Ed Vulliamy, "Will Covid Change Italy?" *New York Review of Books*, September 24, 2020.

73   **Olivia Troye:** Interviewed by video and phone, June 15 and July 7, 2021. Additional details for this section drawn from Yasmeen Abutaleb and Damian Paletta, *Nightmare Scenario* (HarperCollins, 2021). Details include the aborted plan to distribute masks to every American (pp. 184–187). While Troye said she resigned her White House position, others claimed she was forced out.

75   **The delay, experts agreed, cost thousands of lives:** J. David Goodman, "How Delays and Unheeded Warnings Hindered New York's Virus Fight," *New York Times*, April 8, 2020.

76   **hospitals being built in Central Park:** "Samaritan's Purse, in Collaboration with Mount Sinai Health System, Opens Emergency Field Hospital in New York's Central Park in Response to the

Coronavirus Pandemic," Mount Sinai press release, April 1, 2020.

77 **Patrícia Campos Mello dubbed the "hate machine":** "Brazil's Troll Army Moves Into the Streets," *New York Times*, August 4, 2020.

77 **"Nobody should forget that I'm the president":** Gabriel Stargardter and Lisandra Paraguassu, "One Brazilian Minister Shines as Coronavirus Clobbers Bolsonaro," Reuters, April 1, 2020.

77 **While Mandetta's approval rating at the time of his departure stood at 76 percent:** "Brazil Health Minister's Popularity Soars as Bolsonaro's Slips to 33%—Poll," Reuters, April 3, 2020. In May 2021, the Brazilian Senate opened an investigation into President Jair Bolsonaro's mishandling of the country's COVID response. The first witness called to testify was Luiz Henrique Mandetta, in his capacity as the former health minister. Mandetta told senators that he was forced out after failing to accede to Bolsonaro's demands to certify hydroxychloroquine as a COVID treatment. In October, the Senate issued its finding in a 1,300-page report, which recommended that Bolsonaro be charged with nine offenses, including crimes against humanity, for his alleged policy of letting the virus rage unchecked in an effort to achieve herd immunity. The report was referred to Brazil's Prosecutor-General, Augusto Aras, a Bolsonaro appointee. Mandetta, meanwhile, declared that he would be a candidate for president. Elections were scheduled for October 2022. See "'I warned Bolsonaro,' ex-Brazil minister testifies in COVID probe," Al Jazeera, May 4, 2021; "Bolsonaro may face criminal charges for botching COVID response over 'false dilemma,'" NewsHour, October 27, 2021; "Brazil Senators Back Criminal Charges Against Bolsonaro over Covid Handling," BBC, October 27, 2021.

78 **the WHO published a guidance to governments:** "Managing Epidemics: Key Facts About Major Deadly Diseases," 2018.

CHAPTER FOUR

80 Background on dangers of persisting surveillance: Binoy Kampmark, "The Pandemic Surveillance State: An Enduring Legacy of COVID-19," *Journal of Global Faultline* 7, No. 1 (June–August 2020), pp. 59–70.

83 **curbed everything from street crime to spitting, littering and jaywalking:** Elle Metz, "Why Singapore banned chewing gum," BBC News, March 28, 2015.

83 TraceTogether and Singapore's contract tracing efforts: Mia Sato, "Singapore's Police Now Have

176   Access to Contact Tracing Data,"
          MIT Technology Review, January 5,
          2021.

83   **the Exposure Notifications
     System, which has been adopted
     in some forty countries:** Mishaal
     Rahman, XDA, February 25, 2021.

85   **had already done so in one
     murder probe:** Philip Heijmans,
     "Singapore Used Contact Tracing
     Data in Case Involving Murder,"
     Bloomberg, January 5, 2021.

87   **Police have already knocked:**
     Tom Bateman, "Coronavirus: Israel
     Turns Surveillance Tools on Itself,"
     BBC, May 12, 2020.

88   **"All conversations, all text
     messages, all locations, all the
     time":** "The 'Tool' Has Been
     Revealed: The GSS 'Secret Database
     That Collects Your Text Messages,
     Calls and Locations," *Yediot
     Ahronot,* March 27, 2020.

89   **HaMagen:** Allison Kaplan
     Sommer, "Israel Unveils Open
     Source App to Warn Users of
     Coronavirus Cases," Haaretz,
     March 23, 2020.

89   **deployment among the
     million ultra-Orthodox Jews:**
     Gilad Malach and Lee Cahaner,
     "2019 Statistical Report on
     Ultra-Orthodox Society in Israel:
     Highlights," Israel Democracy
     Institute, December 24, 2019.

90   **the State Comptroller's
     Office issued a damning interim
     report:** "Israel: Regulation of
     COVID-19 Digital Contact
     Tracing," Library of Congress,
     December 2020.

91   **worth \$3.6 billion by research
     firm MarketsandMarkets:**
     Joel Schectman, Christopher
     Bing, and Jack Stubbs, "Special
     Report: Cyber-intel Firms Pitch
     Governments on Spy Tools to Trace
     Coronavirus," Reuters April 28,
     2020.

92   **At least eight surveillance
     and cyber-intelligence firms have
     tried to sell their repurposed
     wares to track the pandemic:**
     Joel Schectman, Christopher
     Bing, and Jack Stubbs, "Special
     Report: Cyber-intel Firms Pitch
     Governments on Spy Tools to Trace
     Coronavirus."

92   **More than fifty countries
     deployed smartphone apps:**
     Adrian Shahbaz and Allie Funk,
     "Freedom on the Net 2020, the
     Pandemic's Digital Shadow,"
     Freedom House, October 12, 2020.
     The ground for yet more state
     and corporate surveillance was
     tilled long before COVID-19. In
     exchange for "free" services such
     as email and maps, people give up
     mountains of personal data to tech
     giants that exploit it to generate
     billions of dollars in advertising
     revenue. Consumers cast a long

digital shadow as they click through the enticing offerings of the online world of "surveillance capitalism." Data is hoovered up and sold to commercial advertisers and brokers. Companies that offer information services to security and police forces merge all these data streams into a single system. This is known as data fusion and is offered by US firms such as Palantir, which made headlines in 2019 with its work for US Immigration and Customs Enforcement. It creates powerful information hubs for security services and government agencies to share intelligence that might otherwise be siloed. Police and security agencies not only have the ability to follow the digital trail we leave by using the services of telecom companies, social media platforms, ecommerce, and banking. They can actively deploy intrusive technologies to track us the moment we step outside through CCTV cameras on the ground and in the air, AI-enabled facial recognition software and thermal imaging scanners in the street and shopping centers, automated license plate readers in police cars and on street poles, and mobile cell-site simulators (also known as Stingrays) that trick phones into connecting with them rather than a regular cell tower. It is axiomatic that all this data is up for grabs in a dictatorship. In a democracy, by contrast,

citizens trust that data collection and use would be regulated and enjoy some judicial oversight. But revelations by former US National Security Agency contractor Edward Snowden make clear that if a government really wants information, it will get it.

92   includes a burgeoning DNA databank: The pandemic also raised fears about the possibility of mass DNA collection outside of criminal investigations. Even before COVID, China had begun collecting genetic data from millions of men not just as part of its well-documented repression of Muslim Uighurs in Xinjiang province but as a wider program of genetic mass surveillance. For background on the country's use of DNA surveillance, see Emile Dirks and Dr. James Leibold, "Genomic Surveillance: Inside China's DNA Dragnet," June 17, 2020.

The authors of the Australian report also warned in a July 24, 2020, *New York Times* article that law enforcement and governments everywhere are pushing the ethical boundaries of genetic data collection. "For now, China appears to be the only country in the world where police are harvesting en masse DNA samples outside the scope of criminal investigations. But how much longer before others follow suit?" they asked. See Emile Dirks and James Leibold, "China Is

178   Harvesting the DNA of Its People. Is This the Future of Policing?" *New York Times*, July 24, 2020.

Working with the Beijing government is BGI Group, a Chinese biomedical and gene-sequencing company. When the first COVID cases were detected in the US in Washington State in March 2020, BGI reached out to state officials with an "enticing" offer to build and run COVID testing labs, according to a CBS *60 Minutes* report. The company made similar offers to five other US states including New York and California. See Jon Wertheim, "China's Push to Control America's Health Care Future," *CBS 60 Minutes*, January 31, 2021.

Bill Evanina, then a senior counterintelligence officer, was so alarmed by BGI's ties to the Chinese Communist Party and military that he authorized a rare public warning: "Foreign powers can collect, store and exploit biometric information from COVID tests." No US states took up the BGI offer.

93   **"Close Contact Detector":** "China Launches Coronavirus 'Close Contact Detector' App," BBC, February 11, 2020.

93   **Some apps gave users green, yellow, and red health codes:** Paul Mozur, Raymond Zhong, and Aaron Krolik, "In Coronavirus Fight, China Gives Citizens a Color Code, with Red Flags," *New York Times*, March 1, 2020.

93   **the Alipay Health Code app shared information with the police:** Paul Mozur, Raymond Zhong, and Aaron Krolik, "In Coronavirus Fight, China Gives Citizens a Color Code, with Red Flags."

94   **The government published some of this data, anonymized, on websites and via text messages to alert the public:** Eun-Young Jeong, "South Korea Tracks Virus Patients' Travels—and Publishes Them Online," *Wall Street Journal*, February 16, 2020.

94   **Saudi Arabia, Bahrain, and Qatar:** "Freedom on the Net 2020, Pandemic's Digital Shadow," Freedom House, October 12, 2020.

95   **The southern Indian state of Karnataka required those in self-isolation to send a selfie:** Pallavi Pundir, "Coronavirus Is Pushing Mass Surveillance in India, and It's Going to Change Everything," Vice, April 6, 2020.

95   **Poland and Russia had similar regulations:** "Freedom on the Net 2020, the Pandemic's Digital Shadow," Freedom House, October 12, 2020; "'Selfie app' to keep track of quarantined Poles," France 24, March 20, 2020.

95   **grabbed for intrusive technology:** Sara Garcia and Rory McClaren, "How Will South Australia's Home Quarantine Trial Work?" ABC News, August 23, 2021.

95   **Conor Friedersdorf:** "Australia Traded Away Too Much Liberty," *The Atlantic*, September 2, 2021.

96   **DP-3T:** "Freedom on the Net 2020, The Pandemic's Digital Shadow," Freedom House, October 12, 2020.

96   **Apple and Google developed a notification system for their respective iOS and Android devices:** Darrell Etherington, "Apple and Google Launch Exposure Notification API, Enabling Public Health Authorities to Release Apps," TechCrunch, May 20, 2020.

96   **Failure to install the app was punishable with a fine of up to $55,000 or three years in prison:** "Qatar Makes COVID-19 App Mandatory, Experts Question Efficiency," Al Jazeera, May 26, 2020.

97   Background on Norway's Smittestopp app and concerns over other countries' contact tracking technologies: Natasha Singer, "Virus-Tracing Apps Are Rife with Problems," *New York Times*, July 8, 2020.

99   **Cambridge Analytica:** Matthew Rosenberg and Gabriel J.X. Dance, "'You Are the Product': Targeted by Cambridge Analytica on Facebook," *New York Times*, April 8, 2018.

100   **Political institutions, laws, societal norms, and bioethics have not kept pace with the technology:** Jessica Rich, "How Our Outdated Privacy Laws Doomed Contact-Tracing Apps," Brooking Institution's Techtank, January 28, 2021.

101   **More than 130 countries have some form of constitutional safeguards or regulations on privacy or data protection:** "What Is Privacy?" Privacy International, October 23, 2017.

CHAPTER FIVE

104   **his wife, Rebecca:** Today Rebecca Loftus is a lecturer at ASU, and teaches courses on sex offenders and sex crimes. She is also co-director, along with her husband, of the Israel Counter-Terrorism Study Abroad program that takes students to Israel each summer.

104   **including a case against Western Union:** "Western Union to Pay $94 Mln in Laundering Probe," Reuters, February 11, 2020.

104   **who went by Eddie:** Obituary for Edward Loftus, July 13, 2014.

105   On Loftus's political views: While Loftus dismissed the Birther debate as irrelevant and had few issues with Obamacare, Obama's association with Bill Ayers troubled Loftus greatly. Ayers was one of the founders of the Weathermen,

180   a radical leftist organization that used violence to express its opposition to the war in Vietnam. Ayers had gone on to become a university professor in Chicago, where he ran in Obama's social circles. While Loftus agreed with Trump's immigration policies, he did not like his "in-your-face" approach and felt he sometimes went too far in his language. Loftus believes that "98 percent" of Mexican immigrants cross the border for better wages and not to commit crimes. But the small percentage who are involved in drug trafficking and human smuggling pose a significant threat to public safety in Arizona. Loftus also supports a path to citizenship for Dreamers, immigrants who came to the US as children.

106   **"a member of the ASU community":** Meg O'Connor, "ASU Coronavirus Patient Cleared, Released from Isolation," *Phoenix New Times*, February 21, 2020.

106   Loftus on mask-wearing: While Loftus believes that mask-wearing is of limited utility from a health perspective, he wore a mask himself as an extra precaution. He also did not object to the Arizona mask mandate because it was a way to preserve social harmony in the state at a time when conflicts between those who wore masks and those who refused to do so were rising.

106   **atovaquone/proguanil:** While Loftus described atovaquone/proguanil (which goes by the brand name Malarone) as "a newer version of hydroxychloroquine," in fact it's a different class of drug. When he took Malarone based on Trump's admonitions, Loftus had no way to know if it would be efficacious and compared his decision to playing the lottery, noting, "If you don't play, you don't win." As it turns out, he may have drawn a lucky ticket. A preliminary study published in October 2021 found Malarone "potently inhibits the replication of SARS-CoV-2 and other variants of concern including the alpha, beta, and delta variants." See "Study Finds FDA-approved drug has potent antiviral activity against SARS-CoV-2 and variants of concern," News Medical Life Sciences, October 25, 2021.

107   **"We are fighting an infodemic":** Bill Chappell, "U.N. Chief Targets 'Dangerous Epidemic of Misinformation' on Coronavirus," NPR, April 14, 2020. Transcript of Guterres's February 15 speech at Munich Security Conference, https://www.who.int/director-general/speeches/detail/munich-security-conference.

107   **"Around the world, people are scared":** "'This Is a Time for Facts, Not Fear,' Says WHO Chief

as COVID-19 Virus Spreads," UN News, February 15, 2020.

109   Group identity may be more important than an objective analysis of the facts: Max Fisher, "'Belonging Is Stronger Than Facts': The Age of Misinformation," *New York Times*, May 7, 2021.

109   Pew Research Center: Amy Mitchell, Mark Jurkowitz, J. Baxter Oliphant, and Elisa Shearer, "How Americans Navigated the News in 2020: A Tumultuous Year in Review," Pew Research Center, February 22, 2021.

109   Other studies: Christopher Ingraham, "New Research Explores How Conservative Media Misinformation May Have Intensified the Severity of the Pandemic," *Washington Post*, June 25, 2020.

110   Fox viewers were considerably less likely: Andrey Simonov et al., "The Persuasive Effect of Fox News: Non-Compliance with Social Distancing During the Pandemic," National Bureau of Economic Research, May 2020.

110   poll commissioned by The Knight Foundation and Gallup: Zacc Ritter, "Republicans Still Skeptical of COVID-19 Lethality," Knight Foundation, May 26, 2020. See also, "Amid Pandemic, News Attention Spikes; Media Favorability Flat," *Gallop blog*, April 9, 2020.

111   According to the account of Brian Stelter: Brian Stelter, *Hoax* (Atria/One Signal, 2020), pp. 268–274.

111   Shepard Smith: Smith, who Loftus compared to Walter Cronkite, left Fox News in October 2019, before the start of the pandemic. Nearly a year later, he launched a nightly news show on CNBC, *The News with Shephard Smith*. In an interview with Christiane Amanpour on January 19, 2021, Smith lashed out at his former colleagues. "If you feel like the Fox viewers were getting mis- or disinformation, I was there to make sure that they got it straight," Smith explained. "I believe that when people begin with a false premise and lead people astray, that's injurious to society, and it's the antithesis of what we should be doing." As a matter of disclosure, it should be noted that Smith donated $500,000 to the authors' organization, the Committee to Protect Journalists, in November 2019. See Jake Lahut, "'I Don't Know How Some People Sleep At Night': Former Fox News Host Shepard Smith Unloads on the Network, Calling Out Those Who 'Propagated the Lies,'" *Business Insider*, January 19, 2021. See also Alexis Benveniste, "Shep Smith Breaks His Silence About Why He

182 Left Fox News," CNN, January 20, 2021.

111 Chris Wallace grill Trump: Justin Baragona, "Trump Shrugs Off COVID Death Toll in Fox News Interview: 'It Is What It Is,'" Daily Beast, July 19, 2020.

112 Ingraham (who called hydroxychloroquine a "game changer"): Michael M. Grynbaum, "Fox News Stars Trumpeted a Malaria Drug, Until They Didn't," *New York Times*, April 22, 2020.

113 Joan Donovan, an expert on disinformation: Brian Stelter, "Dr. Joan Donovan on 'Media Manipulation,' the Meme Wars, and How Disinformation Hijacks Free Expression," *Reliable Sources*, CNN, May 21, 2021.

114 Background on the anti-mask movement: Luke Mogelson, "The Militias Against Masks," *New Yorker*, August 17, 2020.

114 Guy Phillips tore a mask from his face, declaring "I can't breathe": Lorraine Longhi, "Scottsdale Councilman Uses Words of George Floyd to Protest Masks," *Arizona Republic*, June 24, 2020.

114 Fox Decision Desk called Arizona: Annie Karni and Maggie Haberman, "Fox's Arizona Call for Biden Flipped the Mood at Trump Headquarters," *New York Times*, November 4, 2020.

115 Arizona saw a massive surge in COVID infections: Stephanie Innes, "Arizona Has the Highest Rate of New COVID-19 Cases in the US, CDC says," *Arizona Republic*, January 4, 2021.

115 Adrian Fontes: Interviewed by phone, January 27, 2021.

117 For more information on the Richer/Fontes election and legal challenges from Republicans: Jen Fifield, "Stephen Richer Unseats Maricopa County Recorder Adrian Fontes for Key Election Post," *Arizona Republic*, November 12, 2020.

118 Chris Stirewalt: "I called Arizona for Biden on Fox News. Here's What I Learned," *Los Angeles Times*, January 28, 2021.

119 Antifa: On March 2, 2021, FBI director Christopher Wray told the US Senate Judiciary Committee, "We have not to date seen any evidence of any anarchist violent extremists or people subscribing to Antifa in connection with the Sixth." See Sarah Lynch, "No Evidence U.S. Capitol Rioters Belong to Antifa Movement, FBI Chief Wray Testifies," Reuters, March 2, 2021. See also Davey Alba, "No, There Is No Evidence That Antifa Activists Stormed the Capitol," *New York Times*, January 6, 2021, and Amanda Macias, "FBI Says There Is 'No Indication' That Antifa Took Part in U.S. Capitol Riot," CNBC, January 8, 2021.

119   **Nancy Pelosi:** Loftus said he saw reports that Nancy Pelosi had ordered the shooting of Ashli Babbitt in a closed group on Parler accessible only to current and former law enforcement personnel. Parler gained a following among conservatives as a "free-speech alternative" to Twitter and Facebook at a time when both were increasingly removing mis- and disinformation. Because participants in the Capitol Hill riot allegedly used Parler to coordinate their actions, the app came under enormous public scrutiny and pressure. Within days of the January 6 assault, Apple and Google removed Parler from their app stores, and Amazon banned it from its server because the site was insufficiently moderating content. A month later, after finding a new hosting service, Parler announced it was back online.

119   **social media platforms did move away:** Jack Nicas and Davey Alba, "Amazon, Apple and Google Cut Off Parler, an App That Drew Trump Supporters," *New York Times*, January 9, 2021. See also Adi Robertson, "Parler Is Back Online After a Month of Downtime," *The Verge*, February 15, 2021.

120   **As Zeynep Tufekci noted:** Zeynep Tufekci, "How Social Media Took Us from Tahrir Square to Donald Trump," *MIT Technology Review*, August 14, 2018.

120   **Emily Bell, director of the Tow Center at Columbia Journalism School:** Interviewed by video, June 17, 2021.

CHAPTER SIX

123   For more detail on *Zeta* and Blancornelas: Joel Simon, "Defending Vanguard Journalists" in *Media Capture: How Money, Digital Platforms, and Governments Control the News*, Anya Schriffin, ed. (Columbia University Press, 2021).

123   Threats against *Zeta*: "Carta al gobernador de Baja California: Preocupante los ataques contra la prensa y libertad de expresión en la entidad," Article 19, July 15, 2020.

123   **State Secretary Amador Rodríguez Lozano lashed out:** "Ofrece disculpa Secretario de Gobierno a periodista Adela Navarro #MochesDelBienestar," Periodismo Negro, December 7, 2019.

124   **hugs and kisses to his supporters:** Jihan Abdalla, "Local Mexico Gov'ts Ramp Up COVID-19 Responses as AMLO Holds Back," Al Jazeera, March 24, 2020.

124   **The livestream was watched by millions of AMLO's supporters:** "Mexican President's Weekday Morning Show Proves an Effective Tool to Reach the Country," Associated Press, January 4, 2021.

184

125 **after the president himself contracted COVID:** Mary Beth Sheridan and Kevin Sieff, "Mexican President Tests Positive for the Coronavirus, Says He Has 'Light' Symptoms," *Washington Post*, January 24, 2021.

125 Bonilla background: Bonilla was a strange bedfellow for MORENA, which was born as a leftist alternative to Mexico's long-ruling Institutional Revolutionary Party, or PRI. Bonilla, a dual citizen of both Mexico and the US, was a registered Republican. He had to abandon his US citizenship to run for governor.

125 **Their analysis revealed a spike in the deaths classified as "atypical pneumonia":** "Baja California, sin atención oportuna a pacientes de COVID-19," *Zeta*, April 3, 2020. Tweet from Adela Navarro Bello: https://twitter.com /adelanavarro/status/12472972582 12585474?s=20.

126 **Mexican government was forced to adjust its system for classifying cases:** Juan Montes, "Death Certificates Point to Much Higher Coronavirus Toll in Mexico," *Wall Street Journal*, May 8, 2020.

126 **thirteen of *Zeta*'s fifty-five employees came down with COVID:** Personal communication, Adela Navarro, February 22, 2021.

126 **Their circulation dropped from a high of 50,000 a week in the 1990s:** personal communication, Adela Navarro, February 22, 2021.

128 **In March 2020, people around the world wanted firsthand, accurate, and timely reporting:** "The search for reliable information related to the pandemic has driven trust in news sources to an all-time high. Traditional media (+7 points) and owned media (+8) saw the biggest gains. Despite these high levels of trust in news sources, there is an urgent need for credible and unbiased journalism. Concerns about fake news still loom large, with 67 percent of respondents worried about false and inaccurate information being spread about the virus." Edelman Trust Barometer, Spring 2020.

128 **"censorship through noise":** McKay Coppins, "The Billion-Dollar Disinformation Campaign to Reelect the President," *The Atlantic*, March 2020.

128 **Reuters Institute's 2020 Digital News Report:** Nic Newman with Richard Fletcher, Anne Schulz, Simge Andı, and Rasmus Kleis Nielsen, Digital News Report 2020.

128 **towns and cities with strong local news outlets are better governed:** Andrew Paxman, a professor at the Centro de Investigación y Docencia Económicas (CIDE) in Mexico City

who is cited later in this chapter, interviewed Navarro in 2019 and shared with her the studies about the link between government efficiency and the presence of local media. See Kriston Capps, "The Hidden Costs of Losing Your City's Newspaper," CityLab, May 30, 2018. See also Pengjie Gao et al., "Financing Dies in Darkness? The Impact of Newspaper Closures on Public Finance," *Journal of Financial Economics*, May 15, 2018.

128   **"Local newspapers are basically little machines that spit out healthier democracies":** Joshua Benton, "When Local Newspapers Shrink, Fewer People Bother to Run for Mayor," Nieman Lab, April 9, 2019.

129   **Google and Facebook account for more than 60 percent:** Kurt Wagner, "Digital Advertising in the US Is Finally Bigger Than Print and Television," Recode, February 20, 2019.

129   **the United States has lost a quarter of its newspapers since 2005:** Penelope Muse Abernathy, "News Deserts and Ghost Papers: Will Local News Survive?" Hussman School of Journalism and Media at the University of North Carolina, June 2020.

129   **2,100 titles have folded, leaving at least 1,800 communities without a local newspaper:** Penelope Muse Abernathy, "News Deserts and

Ghost Papers: Will Local News Survive?"

129   **Many of the 6,700 titles that have survived in the United States have been hollowed out:** Penelope Muse Abernathy, "News Deserts and Ghost Papers: Will Local News Survive?"

129   **"an extinction-level event":** Adam Gabbatt, "US Newspapers Face 'Extinction-Level' Crisis as Covid-19 Hits Hard," *The Guardian*, April 9, 2020.

130   **more than ninety US newsrooms disappeared in the year following the outbreak of the virus:** Kristen Hare, "The Coronavirus Has Closed More Than 60 Local Newsrooms Across America. And Counting," Poynter, February 16, 2021.

130   **37,000 employees of US news media companies had been fired, furloughed, or had their pay cut:** Marc Tracy, "News Media Outlets Have Been Ravaged by the Pandemic," *New York Times*, April 4, 2020.

130   **More than 2,000 staff across the UK's national and regional press had been furloughed or had their salaries cut:** Freddy Mayhew and William Turvill, "More Than 2,000 Newspaper Jobs Hit as Hundreds of Publications Across UK Face Covid-19 Cuts," *Press Gazette*, April 16, 2020.

186

130   advertising revenue fell 11.8 percent in 2020: Damian Radcliffe, "The Impact of COVID-19 on Journalism in Emerging Economies and the Global South," Reuters, 2020.

130   Advertising revenue to media outlets plummeted even as demand for their reporting about the virus soared: Megan Graham, "Media Companies Expect a Tough Quarter for TV Advertising, with No Live Sports and Spending Delayed," CNBC, May 8, 2020. "At a time when lots and lots of companies are slashing their ad budgets, or at least pausing them, now the supply of viewing time or ad inventory exceeds the demand from advertisers to fill it," eMarketer analyst Ross Benes told CNBC. "It's great to get people to watch your show, but each viewer is being monetized much lower than they were months ago."

130   advertising revenue plunged 42 percent in the second quarter in 2020: Michael Barthel, Katerina Eva Matsa, and Kirsten Worden, "Coronavirus-Driven Downturn Hits Newspapers Hard as TV News Thrives," Pew Research Center, October 29, 2020.

131   According to the survey group Comscore: Interview with Rasmus Kleis Nielsen, Director of the Reuters Institute for the Study of Journalism and Professor of Political Communication at the University of Oxford: "And one of the reasons why local titles are often finding it quite difficult to find a foothold . . . in a digital media environment is that they account for a tiny fraction of the time that people spend with news and media in the United States. All news and information providers combined, according to Comscore, account for something like 4 percent of time spent online, all local news providers in the US combined is about a half percent."

131   doubled in eighteen European countries: Chris Dziadul, "Public Service Media 'Respond Rapidly' to COVID-19," Broadband TV News, March 24, 2020.

132   20 percent jump in young viewers: Chris Dziadul, "Public Service Media 'Respond Rapidly' to COVID-19." See also "The Financial Impact of Covid-19 on European Public Broadcasters, " Public Media Alliance, May 13, 2020.

132   14 percent on average: Chris Dziadul, "Public Service Media," Broadband TV News, March 24, 2020.

132   plunge by an average of 50 percent in a matter of weeks: Lucy Handley, "Ad Shift from TV to Digital Will Speed Up Even More Because of Coronavirus, Goldman Sachs Says," CNBC, May 26, 2020.

132   **The wasting away of local news outlets had created a vacuum:** Priyanjana Bengani, "As Election Looms, a Network of Mysterious 'Pink Slime' Local News Outlets Nearly Triples in Size," CJR, August 4, 2020.

132   Background on use of disinformation during the pandemic: Michael R. Gordon and Dustin Volz, "Russian Disinformation Campaign Aims to Undermine Confidence in Pfizer, Other Covid-19 Vaccines, U.S. Officials Say," *Wall Street Journal*, March 7, 2021.

133   **average of 50 percent more time on screens:** Julie Bos, "Soaring Screen Time," Vision Monday, September 21, 2020. Vision Monday reported on September 21, 2020, that before the COVID-19 pandemic, the average American surveyed was getting about four hours of screen time per day. Since the quarantine started, that number has jumped up to over six hours—and their eyes are paying the price.

133   **nearly half the people online do not get their information from recognized news sites:** Pew Research Center said on January 12, 2021, that about half of US adults say they get news from social media "often" or "sometimes," and this use is spread out across a number of different sites. Facebook stands out as a regular source of news for about a third of Americans. See "News

Use Across Social Media Platforms in 2020," Pew Research Center, January 12, 2021.

133   **US Bureau of Labor statistics:** Rasmus Kleis Nielsen, "The Changing Economic Contexts of Journalism," chapter in the *Handbook of Journalism Studies*, 2nd ed., eds. Karin Wahl-Jorgensen and Thomas Hanitzsch (Routledge, 2019).

134   **the corresponding figures were 69 percent, 10 percent, and just 1 percent:** Rasmus Kleis Nielsen, "The Changing Economic Contexts of Journalism."

134   **Brazil . . . is riddled with news deserts:** "The News Deserts in Brazil," Projor, May 2020.

135   **60 percent of people do not have internet access:** Nzekwe Henry, "Only 33% of Africa Is Online, 60% Of Nigerians Lack Internet, Just 10% Are Active on Social Media—Report," WeeTracker, January 31, 2020.

135   **Ntibinyane Ntibinyane:** Martina Bertam, "Digitization Without Monetization: African News Media Stuck Between a Rock and a Hard Place," Deutsche Welle, August 6, 2020.

136   **In France, Google agreed in January 2021:** Helene Fouquet, "Google Signs Deal with French Media to Pay for Content," Bloomberg News, January 21, 2021.

188

136 **Australia where the government strong-armed tech platforms:** Daniel Van Boom and Queenie Wong, "Australia Passes Law Forcing Google and Facebook to Pay News Publications," C-Net, February 21, 2021.

136 **News Media and Digital Platforms Mandatory Bargaining Code:** "News Media Bargaining Code: Project Overview," Australian Competition & Consumer Commission.

137 **worth a total of $47 million:** Daniel Van Boom and Queenie Wong, "Australia Passes Law Forcing Google and Facebook to Pay News Publications."

137 **have accepted government subsidies:** Daniel LeBlanc, "Media Sector Gets $595-Million Package in Ottawa's Fiscal Update," *The Globe and Mail*, November 21, 2018.

137 **strengthened their subscriber base:** Sara Fischer, "Trump Bump: NYT and WaPo Digital Subscriptions Tripled Since 2016," Axios, November 4, 2020; Richard Milne, "Swedish Newspaper Eyes Best Financial Result This Century," *Irish Times*, September 29, 2020; "2020: Pivotal Year in the Digital Transformation of Mediahuis," Mediahuis Group Communications; "Le Monde: Le Million D'Abonnés Numériques Fin 2023," AFP, December 7, 2020; Tara Kelly, "Two Months, a Voluntary 30% Price Increase and

18,000 New Paying Readers: What Eldiario.es Did After COVID-19 Struck," Poynter, May 28, 2020; Sherwin Chua, "How Publishers Are Developing Sustainable Post-COVID-19 Reader Revenue Strategies," World Association of News Publishers, July 28, 2020; Tom Gosling, "A Model for Survival? Online Subscriptions Help Denník N Weather Pandemic," International Press Institute, October 16, 2020.

138 **Martha Minow:** Interview conducted via email with Robert Mahoney, July 13, 2021. For more on this argument, see Martha Minow, *Saving the News: Why the Constitution Calls for Government Action to Preserve Freedom of Speech* (Oxford University Press, 2021).

139 **Canada has an income tax credit for local news subscribers:** Marie-Danielle Smith, "Liberals unveil tax breaks for media companies—and subscribers," Financial Post, March 19, 2019.

139 **France . . . introduced a similar income tax credit:** Jon Henley, "France gives tax credits to news subscribers in effort to rescue sector," *The Guardian*, July 1, 2020.

139 **give Americans $250 to buy local news subscriptions:** "H.R.7640—Local Journalism Sustainability Act," 116th Congress, July 16, 2021. The Local Journalism Sustainability Act allows individual and business taxpayers certain

tax credits for the support of local newspapers and media. Specifically, individual taxpayers may claim an income tax credit up to $250 for a local newspaper subscription. See also Steve Waldman, "Why Local News Should Be Included in the Infrastructure Bill," Poynter, May 28, 2021.

140 **The International Fund for Public Interest Media:** "The fund," International Fund for Public Interest Media, 2021. The principal role of the International Fund for Public Interest Media is to enable media to work for democracy. It will support the media through this time of existential threat and develop lasting solutions to the current media market failure in low- and middle-income countries.

141 **Former Trump strategist Steve Bannon cynically called it "flood the zone with shit":** Sean Illing, "'Flood the Zone with Shit': How Misinformation Overwhelmed Our Democracy," Vox, February 6, 2020.

CHAPTER SEVEN

142 **Zhang Zhan:** Vivian Wang, "She Chronicled China's Crisis. Now She Is Accused of Spreading Lies," *New York Times*, December 25, 2020.

143 **subjected to forced psychological examination:** Radio Free Asia, November 26, 2019.

143 Zhang's YouTube channel: https://www.youtube.com /channel/UCsNKkvZGMURF mYkfhYa2HOQ/videos.

143 **condemned her to four years in prison:** https://twitter .com/IanEverhart/status /1328221139571789824/photo/1; https://twitter.com/IanEverhart /status/1328221139571789824 /photo/2; https://twitter.com /IanEverhart/status/132822113 9571789824/photo/3.

143 **China has invested a fortune in new measures to monitor and control online speech:** Raymond Zhong, Paul Mozur, Jeff Kao, and Aaron Krolik, "No 'Negative' News: How China Censored the Coronavirus," *New York Times*, December 19, 2020.

144 **Jimmy Lai:** "Hong Kong Police Charge Apple Daily Founder Jimmy Lai with 'Foreign Collusion' Under National Security Law," CPJ, December 11, 2020. See also Austin Ramzy, "Hong Kong Court Sentences Jimmy Lai and Other Pro-Democracy Leaders to Prison," *New York Times*, April 16, 2021.

144 **WHO delegation:** Javier C. Hernández, "China Scores a Public Relations Win After W.H.O. Mission to Wuhan," *New York Times*, February 9, 2021; Jeremy Page, Betsy McKay, and Drew Hinshaw, "How the WHO's Hunt for Covid's Origins Stumbled

190 in China," *Wall Street Journal*, March 17, 2021.

146 **"Democracy Under Lockdown":** Sarah Repucci and Amy Slipowitz, "Democracy Under Lockdown," Freedom House, October 2020.

147 **annual Freedom in the World survey:** Repucci and Slipowitz, "Democracy Under Siege," Freedom House, March 2021.

148 **"the democratic recession began":** Larry Diamond, "Democratic Regression in Comparative Perspective: Scope, Methods, and Causes," *Democratization* (July 31, 2020), pp. 22–42.

148 **Varieties of Democracy research project:** "V-Dem: Global Standards, Local Knowledge," V-Dem Institute.

149 **Maria Ressa:** Sheila Coronel, "This Is How Democracy Dies," *The Atlantic*, June 16, 2020. Personal communication, September 5, 2021.

149 **granted him sweeping temporary emergency powers:** "Asia Today: Duterte Extends Virus Calamity Status by a Year," Associated Press, September 21, 2020.

149 **Duterte's loyal legislature granted him sweeping emergency powers:** Sofia Tomacruz, "Duterte Signs Law Granting Himself Special Powers to Address Coronavirus Outbreak," Rappler, March 24, 2020.

149 **Philippine Anti-Terrorism Act, which allows:** Julie McCarthy, "Why Rights Groups Worry About the Philippines' New Anti-Terrorism Law," NPR, July 21, 2020.

150 **Sophie Wilmès:** Former prime minister and later foreign minister Sophie Wilmès sent written answers to interview questions on March 10, 2021.

151 **of the eighty-three countries that restricted fundamental democratic rights:** "Covid-19 Triggers Wave of Free Speech Abuse," Human Rights Watch, February 11, 2021.

152 ***Jacobson v. Commonwealth of Massachusetts:*** *Jacobson v. Com. of Massachusetts* (1905) No. 70. Argued December 6, 1904. Decided February 20, 1905.

153 Jacobson's legacy: James Colgrove and Ronald Bayer, "Manifold Restraints: Liberty, Public Health, and the Legacy of Jacobson *v* Massachusetts," *American Journal of Public Health*, November 16, 2004.

153 **The AIDS epidemic of the 1980s and 1990s:** Colgrove and Bayer, "Manifold Restraints," *American Journal of Public Health*, November 16, 2004.

154   Background on correlation between COVID effectiveness and democracy: The Australia-based Lowy Institute created an interactive database called the COVID Performance Index that sought to link the effectiveness of a country's response to COVID with a variety of factors, including its political system, its population size, and its level of economic development. Based on data available as of January 2021, researchers found almost no correlation between COVID effectiveness and democracy, with democratic countries at the top (New Zealand), the bottom (Brazil), and sprinkled throughout. Likewise, autocratic countries were scattered from top to bottom, with no correlation to effective outcomes. The report found that "levels of economic development or differences in political systems between countries had less of an impact on outcomes than often assumed or publicized." See also, Thomas J. Bollyky, Sawyer Crosby, and Samantha Kiernan, "Fighting a Pandemic Requires Trust," *Foreign Affairs*, October 23, 2020.

Columbia Global Reports is a publishing imprint from Columbia University that commissions authors to do original on-site reporting around the globe on a wide range of issues. The resulting novella-length books offer new ways to look at and understand the world that can be read in a few hours. Most readers are curious and busy. Our books are for them.

Subscribe to our newsletter, and learn more about Columbia Global Reports at globalreports.columbia.edu.